THE KIT
FURNITURE BOOK

THE KIT
FURNITURE BOOK

LYNDA GRAHAM-BARBER

PANTHEON BOOKS ⛪ NEW YORK

**In loving memory of my grandmothers,
Bertha Billick and Martha Pascoe**

*Portions of this book have previously appeared in some-
what different form in* The New York Times *and*
McCall's.
*Grateful acknowledgment is made to The Taunton Press,
Inc., for permission to reprint the recipe for milk paint.
Copyright © 1981 The Taunton Press, Inc. Reprinted from*
Fine Woodworking, *No. 27.*

No manufacturer has been paid to be included in
The Kit Furniture Book.

Library of Congress Cataloging in Publication Data

*Graham-Barber, Lynda.
The kit furniture book.
Bibliography: p.
1. Furniture making—Amateurs' manuals.
I. Title.
TT195.G73   684.1'04   81-48252
ISBN 0-394-70674-9 (pbk.) AACR2*

Manufactured in the United States of America
First Edition

PERSONAL ACKNOWLEDGMENTS

I would like to extend grateful and warmest thanks to Todd Shearer for his splendid work as photo stylist; Michel Legrou and Marc Weinstein for their superb photography; Betsy Amster, my editor, for her advice and support; Robin Stevens, assistant editor, for her careful attention to detail; Gayle Benderoff and Deborah Geltman, my literary agents, for shepherding this project with care and enthusiasm; Ken Schroeder, Dick Dabrowski, and Mary Hagerty for their valued assistance; and, most important, Ray Barber, whose tireless and inspired guidance enriched and expedited every phase in the preparation of this book.

CONTENTS

THE KIT
FURNITURE BOOK

INTRODUCTION

My husband and I became kit enthusiasts as early as 1974, at a time when it was probably considered somewhat revolutionary—and certainly unorthodox—to buy furniture in unassembled and unfinished form. One didn't order serious furniture like beds and chairs in pieces from mail-order catalogs and glue them together. One bought furniture, usually in suites, in stores and waited a minimum of six weeks for delivery.

When I assembled the seven parts of that first kit—a maple candle stand I'd seen advertised in a magazine, modeled after one in the Metropolitan Museum of Art—it was my maiden foray into the woodworking field. To my surprise and delight, all the parts fitted together neatly, the finish—which was provided—went on evenly, and the only tool I needed was a hammer. That first kit is still with us, sitting in the hallway, topped by an antique bowl and pitcher. It was inexpensive then and still is today, selling for a modest $28.00—less than the price of lunch for two at many New York City restaurants.

We followed the candle stand with nine more kits in Colonial, Shaker, and Queen Anne styles. Our canopy bed, dining-room table and chairs, dresser, and even medicine chest were assembled from mail-order kits. Our most ambitious project to date was a clavichord (nearly 100 couple-hours); the simplest was a country quilt rack that I put together and stained, no gluing required, in an hour.

It may sound like a bit of a potpourri, but the kits worked together marvelously. By the time we were finished, we had furnished our four-room apartment for under $2000.00, a savings of about 60 percent less than finished pieces. We have bought a smattering of antiques since then, but our kits still form the nucleus of our furnishings.

Kit building, like most other building endeavors, is not without risks and frustrations, usually resulting from errors made in haste. I distinctly remember the leg glued on backward, the too-darkly stained end grain on a tabletop, the rush seat that started out perfectly square and ended up perfectly cockeyed. All of these situations could easily have been avoided had we exercised more patience and care.

These pitfalls aside, the old Yankee saying that "He who makes his own is twice rewarded" will become abundantly clear to anyone who builds furniture from kits. The rewards fall into four categories: cost savings, quality,

Cohasset Colonials' candle stand.

INTRODUCTION

convenience, and a sense of accomplishment.

If you've shopped recently for furniture in department or furniture stores, you've undoubtedly noticed shoddy craftsmanship and shortcuts, even on pieces that sell from moderate to high prices. The savings on furniture bought in kit form runs anywhere from 30 to 60 percent. Kits, however, are no exception to the rule that you get what you pay for: price is commensurate with the quality and kind of wood used in the kit, the detail in the design, and whether, for instance, a tabletop is one solid piece of wood or veneered. You can therefore expect to pay up to twice as much for a kit of cherry as for one of pine.

Because the kit buyer is in a position to examine the parts closely before they are assembled, kit sellers are not as likely to use inferior woods or take shortcuts. For sturdiness, joints are often dovetail or mortise-and-tenon, both of which require precision cutting. By contrast, defects and weak joints can easily be concealed in already-assembled furniture, which cannot be scrutinized to such a degree. Some kit companies do use pine that contains a good smattering of knots, to which some people may object. Clear pine is

always defined as such. The companies that use cherry, mahogany, and black walnut in their furniture most often use only the top two grades of lumber (there are five top grades in all).

In addition to the inflated prices and questionable quality of much assembled furniture sold today, there are often annoying delays in delivery. Kit furniture, on the other hand, is shipped (many times within a few days of receipt of order) to your home to be assembled at your convenience. In the case of modern kit furniture (commonly referred to as knockdown or KD), which is sold mostly in retail stores, the pieces can usually be carried out of the store with you since they are packaged in either unassembled or partially assembled units. Chances are good, therefore, that the table kit you ordered by mail, or took home yourself, will be assembled, stained, finished, and in your living area before the furniture-store van arrives with the table you selected on the showroom floor.

The bonus—not to be overlooked—is the enormous sense of pride and accomplishment you'll experience once the furniture is completed. Most of our friends still find it hard to believe that a good portion of our furnishings came unassembled and unfinished.

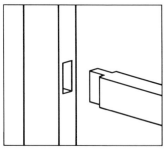

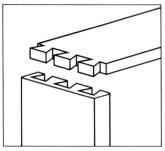

Top: Mortise-and-tenon joint. The mortise is at left, the tenon at right.

Bottom: Dovetail joint.

This book reflects several years of exploration and working with kits. It grew in part out of an article on the subject that I wrote in 1979 for the *Home* section of the *New York Times*. The article provoked an enormous response. The kit companies mentioned were deluged with mail inquiries (one company had to hire trucks to bring the mail from the post office), and I received a flurry of letters from readers asking my advice. Clearly a large percentage of the furniture-buying public was willing to invest time and energy in order to own well-made, solid pieces of furniture instead of shoddily crafted ones that might last two or three years. At the same time, kit manufacturers began to proliferate in response to consumer demand. A book seemed the most practical way to alert people to the variety of kits available and to help them avoid most problems in assembling the furniture they decided to order.

During the two years I researched this book, I scoured magazines for kit companies, made scores of telephone calls, visited manufacturers, talked with company presidents and marketing personnel, met with designers of knockdown furniture and their public-relations firms, and combed stores in the New York area for new KD manufacturers.

At the start, I approached some 100 companies that either produced or sold kits or KD furniture. Of these I narrowed the field to approximately 50. My decision to include these was based on several factors. In 20 or so cases I had had direct involvement with the company's product; I had either assembled a kit prior to this project or did so later. In cases where it was not practical for me to assemble the kits myself, I based my decision on recommendations of individuals in the kit industry whose opinions I came to respect or on comments and tips from friends who had direct experience with certain products. In these instances, I also requested detailed instructions and diagrams of the kits so I could evaluate joinery and wood thicknesses, for example. I also considered how long a company had been in business and how it responded to my queries. I eliminated firms whose representatives reported having difficulty filling orders because of supplier problems, who were elusive about the materials they used, and who seemed wary or uncooperative about supplying detailed information.

The companies represented in the book range from large, well-established firms that publish full-color catalogs,

INTRODUCTION

run ads in major magazines, and operate retail stores to small, family-operated businesses that manufacture perhaps only one or two kit models, advertise sparingly, and work out of the owner's home. For example, one of the newest kit manufacturers, Heath Craft Woodworks (an affiliate of Heathkit Electronics), has about 150 retail stores throughout the country. Paul Saupe, on the other hand, makes Victorian swing rocker kits (based on a chair of his mother's) and sells them by mail order from his Iowa workshop.

In order to guide readers through the range of kits sold today, I have grouped them into four major categories: Colonial (including Windsor), Queen Anne (including Chippendale), Shaker, and contemporary KD pieces. There is, in addition, a brief turn-of-the-century section that features Victorian pieces based on furniture made between 1880 and 1920. There is also a section on clocks and musical instruments and another on kit houses; both represent a sample—not an exhaustive directory—of what the interested buyer can expect to find. An introduction opens each section, giving historical information (if appropriate) on the furniture represented, along with details on the companies producing kits of that type.

I suggest that before you make any decisions on ordering, you browse through the entire book to familiarize yourself with the range of what is available. Furniture has been grouped by type—chairs, tables, chests, and so on—to make selection easier. Next to each photograph appears pertinent information such as the type of wood used, the number of pieces in the kit, assembly time, and price. Captions call attention to design details or differences between similar pieces sold by two different companies.

The step-by-step sections, showing exactly how to assemble a Shaker rocker, a canopy bed, and a blockfront chest, should prove especially helpful to those who have never welcomed the challenge presented by a box full of jigsaw pieces. The color photographs, many shot in our Brooklyn apartment, will give ideas on how kits can be effectively incorporated into a wide variety of decors. The text at the end of the book features tips on gluing, sanding, staining, varnishing, and waxing (and even includes a recipe for mixing your own milk paint). At the very end is a complete directory of the kit and KD companies mentioned in the book, giving addresses and ordering information.

Remember when you compare prices

among manufacturers that the costs of kits are commensurate with quality and materials. For instance, don't expect a cherry Chippendale table with extensive period details and hand-rubbed brass hardware to cost the same as one of the same size but made of pine with few details or little ornament. Bear in mind, too, that although the kit cherry table may cost twice as much as the pine one, a fully assembled cherry table of comparable quality would probably cost even twice again as much in a reputable furniture store.

Similarly, don't be misled by those ubiquitous ads in magazines for $19.00 mahogany tables. They are *not* constructed of the same quality mahogany as pieces available in kit form or from reputable furniture stores. And if you closely examine pine furniture sold in stores specializing in raw or unfinished furniture, I doubt you'll find any dovetail joints typical of pine pieces sold in kit form, which may cost only slightly more.

Kits are contagious, but I can't think of a more rewarding mania to catch. You'll come away from the venture with a newfound awareness of fine craftsmanship and a sharper eye, both of which will stand you in good stead the next time you shop for furniture in stores or go hunting for antiques.

A note about the listings in the catalog sections that follow:

o To help you compare different kits, manufacturers' dimensions have been standardized to read *width* (W) x *depth* (D) x *height* (H), except in the case of beds, where *length* (L) and *width* (W) measurements are used. In general, *width* represents the distance from side to side, while *depth* represents the distance from front to back.

o Number of parts listed does not include sundry parts such as screws.

o Assembly times given will vary according to individual experience and do not include time required for staining and finishing.

o Unless noted, prices listed do not include shipping costs, nor do they necessarily reflect the prices that apply when ordering from Canada.

o Since all prices are subject to change, it's advisable to write for the most current prices before sending any money. In some cases prices may actually be lower; a number of kit companies run sales seasonally.

CATALOG
OF KITS

Kit: Hutch
Period: Eighteenth
  century
Company: Cohasset
  Colonials
Dimensions: 35″W
  x 18 1/2″D x 63 1/2″H
Wood: Pine
Number of parts: 18
Assembly time: 3 hours
Price: $299.00

COLONIAL KITS (1650–1800)

In its strictest sense, the term *colonial* refers to the period before the thirteen colonies declared their independence from Great Britain. Furniture historians, however, almost inevitably extend the period to include furniture designed until at least 1800. This wide umbrella covers such diverse styles as the primitive, unadorned furniture constructed in rural areas to the more sophisticated and refined pieces favored in cities.

Early Colonial furniture was crude and massive, with little attention given to proportion or line. With choice hardwoods difficult to procure, craftsmen worked instead with maple (curly and bird's-eye especially), pine, ash, oak, poplar, and beech, all of which were abundant. Since metal for nails and screws was at first unavailable, and glue was a little-known commodity, furniture was, of necessity, built with skillfully fitted dovetail and dado joints and strong mortise-and-tenon construction, held together with pegs.

Ornamentation in the nascent stages of Colonial design was minimal, consisting of simple turned shapes and applied moldings. But cabinetmakers soon developed uniquely American styles of furniture that compared favorably with those of European origins.

Although Colonial craftsmen were naturally influenced by European styles, the furniture they fashioned showed greater simplicity, usefulness, and clarity of design. Flamboyant details in moldings, carvings, and ornate inlays were refreshingly absent. By comparison, English furniture of the period seems gussied up, almost as if the cabinetmakers decided to try out every curlicue in their vocabulary.

The wood in many early pieces was left raw, darkening with time, touch, and exposure to air. Many cabinetmakers (especially those of German and Scandinavian descent) painted their furniture. Most homemade paints were water soluble, similar to our modern water-based paints, except that they did not contain any synthetic resins and were not mixed in as wide a range of colors. Often called milk paint, buttermilk paint, or refractory paint, Colonial paints were made of skimmed milk, lime whiting, and ground color. The recipes may have been homespun, but the paints endured. It's not unusual to find a Colonial antique today with its original paint still in good condition.

In the latter part of the 1600s, linseed oil and beeswax were introduced as finishing compounds for quality furniture, and shellac appeared at the end of the century. This shellac was formed by dissolving a resinous secretion from a Far Eastern insect in alcohol. The varnish we use today, which consists of resins dissolved in hot oils, appeared in about 1848.

Since the chair was the single most important piece of furniture in the Colonial home, much attention was given to its design. The ladderback, a style still popular today, came into use early; William Penn, in fact, brought a sample with him from England in 1682. These chairs were often painted, then stenciled and striped to accentuate the turnings; in some cases the chairs were stained and then decorated with paint. Seats were woven with rush fibers or with splints—strips of wood, usually hickory or basswood. Other typical chairs included the wainscot chair (named for the wainscot panels found on tavern walls), the Brewster chair, and the banister-back chair. But the most popular Colonial chair of all was undoubtedly the Windsor.

First made in the colonies in Philadelphia around 1725, the model for this lightweight, durable chair supposedly came from Windsor, England, where King George I (reigned 1714–1727) admired one in town and took it back to his castle. George Washington was so enamored of Windsor chairs that he bedecked his portico at Mount Vernon with 30 of them for his guests. Originally made of humble woods—hickory and oak—with pine seats and maple legs, the chairs were considered serviceable above all and usually sat in the front hall of a house, where wet guests were able to dry off before entering the living quarters. The chairs were often painted, with green a favored color. The names of the different styles—for example, low-back, comb-back, hoop-back, and fanback—refer to the various shapes of the spindled back. The most noticeable difference between the English and American Windsor is that the English chair backs generally have a pierced upright splat in the center of the spindles.

A Colonial ladderback chair launched the career of Francis Hagerty, the late founder of Cohasset Colonials. The first kit company in the United States, it was founded in 1938 in Cohasset, Massachusetts. Mr. Hagerty introduced his first line of kits in 1950 (after an interruption for service in World War II) with a catalog of 15 kits and an ad in the *New York Times* featuring his ladderback chair (a copy of one in the Boston Museum of Fine Arts) for $9.95. The same kit now sells for $75.00 from

COLONIAL KITS (1650–1800)

Cohasset—not bad considering that over 30 years have passed.

In the intervening years, Cohasset has added nearly 40 more items to its original line. Nearly all Cohasset pieces are reproductions of originals found in New England museums and historical collections, such as the Metropolitan Museum of Art in New York and Wadsworth Atheneum in Hartford, Connecticut.

Cohasset's distinction of being the lone contender in the kit field did not last long; in 1951, Yield House, in North Conway, New Hampshire, began selling mail-order kits. For over three decades now, these two companies have offered an exhaustive selection of Colonial kits.

Within the past five years, a number of new firms have set up business. Some of these specialize in Colonial chairs, others in accessories. Colonial furniture—especially more primitive pieces called country furniture—has never been more popular, and there are more companies turning out seventeenth- and eighteenth-century kits than of any other period.

Kit fanciers can therefore choose from an enormous variety of Colonial chairs (Windsors of several types, ladderbacks, benches) and tables (trestle, butterfly, tavern, round), as well as more unusual kits such as rag rugs, weathervanes, and rocking horses.

For the most part, kit companies use the woods of the period to fashion their kits—pine, maple, ash, poplar, and cherry. Three different woods make up Cohasset's four-poster canopy bed. Secondary woods (not as attractive) are often used by kit companies in places where they won't be noticed, just as the Colonial woodworkers did.

Yield House gives the customer three options in buying its furniture. The company sells regular kits (wood, glue, and hardware but no stain) that require full assembly, KD pieces (easily assembled, no gluing), and finished pieces that cost about 25 percent more than ones you assemble yourself. Western Reserve Antique Furniture Kit in Bath, Ohio, and The Bartley Collection in Prairie View, Illinois, sell finished kits, but for as much as double the cost of the unassembled pieces. The prices for finished pieces, however, are commensurate with the wood used and the quality of the finish.

When ordering from Colonial kit makers, read their catalogs closely to find out what kind of joinery they employ. If, for example, they use a rabbet (slot for joining corners) in drawer constructions, you may find your drawers more difficult to operate smoothly than if dovetail joints are used—but the cost is likely to be less. If you choose an item made of pine, be certain that parts subject to strain (table legs, for example) are made of a stronger wood such as maple.

Most of the kits included in this section are reproductions of pieces now housed in museums or are closely modeled after drawings of early pieces. Some, although certainly Early American in inspiration, have been adapted and modified to be more compatible with the wide range of contemporary furnishings sold today. The pieces offered by Yield House and American Forest Products exemplify this so-called modernized country look. These two firms offer a number of kits in this style that tend to be quite inexpensive because they are nearly all constructed of pine, usually a knotty grade.

I've tried in the following section to present a diversified selection of what is available in kit form from the rich Colonial period. Interested buyers should also make a point of perusing ads in publications such as *Yankee, Country Journal, Colonial Homes, House Beautiful*, and *Americana* to keep abreast of new kit companies.

Kit: Ladderback side chair
Period: Eighteenth century
Company: Cohasset Colonials
Dimensions: 19 1/2"W x 17"D x 43 1/2"H
Wood: Maple
Number of parts: 14
Assembly time: 5–6 hours including seat rushing
Price: $75.00

This ladderback chair, the one that launched Cohasset's kit line in 1950, is painted and then decorated to accentuate the turnings—a style typical of the colonial period.

Kit: Ladderback armchair
Period: Eighteenth century
Company: Cohasset Colonials
Dimensions: 21 1/2"W x 16 1/2"D x 43 1/2"H
Wood: Maple
Number of parts: 16
Assembly time: 5–6 hours including seat rushing
Price: $87.00

COLONIAL KITS (1650–1800)

Kit: Bowback Windsor side chair
Period: Circa 1740
Company: The Bartley Collection, Ltd.
Dimensions: 21 1/2" square x 38"H
Wood: Ash
Number of parts: 16
Assembly time: 3 1/2 hours
Price: $149.00

The back of this bowback Windsor is formed by a single uninterrupted steam-bent bow that is driven into the seat.

Kit: Hoop-back Windsor armchair
Period: Circa 1740
Company: The Bartley Collection, Ltd.
Dimensions: 24"W x 22"D x 38"H
Wood: Ash
Number of parts: 23
Assembly time: 4 hours
Price: $169.00

This Windsor is also known as a sack-back, supposedly because a sack could be tied to the back of the chair to protect the sitter from rear drafts.

Kit: Windsor armchair
Period: Mid-1700s
Company: The Hardwood Craftsman, Ltd.
Dimensions: 25 1/2"W x 18"D x 34"H
Wood: Birch
Number of parts: 28
Assembly time: 4 hours
Price: $150.00

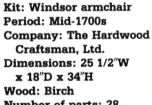

When spindles continue through the arms and end in the comb-top crest rail, the Windsor is called a comb-back. Note the scroll handholds on the ends of the armrests.

Kit: Windsor side chair
Period: Mid-1700s
Company: Cohasset Colonials
Dimensions: 17"W x 16"D x 35 1/2"H
Woods: Maple/pine
Number of parts: 10
Assembly time: 3 hours
Price: $78.00

Note the bamboo turnings on the splayed legs and double rail of the Sheraton-inspired back. The seat is constructed of clear pine.

Kit: Windsor armchair
Period: Mid-1700s
Company: Cohasset Colonials
Dimensions: 21 1/2″W x 17 1/2″D x 35 1/2″H
Woods: Maple/pine
Number of parts: 16
Assembly time: 3 hours
Price: $98.00

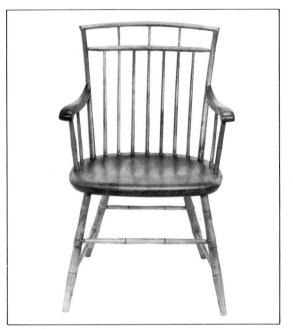

Kit: Settee
Period: Circa 1740
Company: Cohasset Colonials
Dimensions: 44″W x 16 1/2″D x 35 1/2″H
Wood: Pine
Number of parts: 23
Assembly time: 3–4 hours
Price: $173.00

Kit: Child's Windsor rocker (ages 3 to 7)
Period: Circa 1760
Company: Cohasset Colonials
Dimensions: 13 1/4″W x 21 1/2″D x 24″H
Woods: Pine/maple
Number of parts: 23
Assembly time: 3 1/2 hours
Price: $76.00

Kit: Windsor high chair
Period: Mid-1700s
Company: Cohasset Colonials
Dimensions: 13″W x 13″D x 22 1/2″H (seat); 34 1/2″H
Woods: Maple/pine
Number of parts: 16
Assembly time: 2–3 hours
Price: $79.00

It would take a very strong baby to upset this chair with its wide leg angle.

COLONIAL KITS (1650–1800)

Kit: Colonial arrow-back
Period: 1810–1835
Company: Zimmerman
   Chair Shop
Dimensions: 18"W x 17"D
   x 36"H
Woods: Maple; oak; cherry
Number of parts: 16
Assembly time: 2–3 hours
Price: $68.00 maple;
   $80.00 oak and cherry

Kit: Country arrow-back
Period: 1810–1835
Company: Zimmerman
   Chair Shop
Dimensions: 16"W x 15"D
   x 33"H
Woods: Maple; oak; cherry
Number of parts: 16
Assembly time: 2–3 hours
Price: $54.00 maple;
   $59.00 oak and cherry

Kit: Windsor side chair
Period: Circa 1820
Company: The Hardwood
   Craftsman, Ltd.
Dimensions: 19 1/2"W
   x 17 1/2"D x 34 1/2"H
Wood: Oak
Number of parts: 16
Assembly time: 2 1/2
   hours
Price: $125.00

*The simple incised rings on
the splayed legs of this
arrow-back Windsor are a
design simplification of
bamboo turnings.*

Kit: Windsor rocker
Period: Circa 1820
Company: The Hardwood
   Craftsman, Ltd.
Dimensions: 26"W
   x 28 1/2"D x 43 1/2"H
Wood: Birch
Number of parts: 26
Assembly time: 3 1/2
   hours
Price: $145.00

Kit: Captain's chair
Period: Eighteenth
  century
Company: Cohasset
  Colonials
Dimensions: 22″W
  x 15 1/2″D x 28 1/2″H
Woods: Maple/pine
Number of parts: 22
Assembly time: 3 1/2
  hours
Price: $99.00

*This low-back Windsor
(which originated in Rhode
Island) has ornamentally
turned spindles and X-
stretchers. The chair has
been painted and decorated
using Cohasset's stencil kit.*

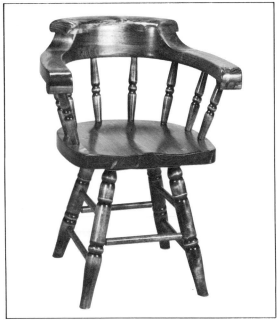

Kit: Captain's chair
Period: Eighteenth
  century
Company: Yield House
Dimensions: 25″W x 21″D
  x 31″H
Woods: Pine seat and
  back; hardwood legs
Number of parts:
  Preassembled, shipped
  knocked down (KD)
Assembly time: 1/2 hour
Price: $119.00

Kit: Mate's chair
Period: Circa 1800
Company: Zimmerman
  Chair Shop
Dimensions: 18″W x 17″D
  x 30″H
Woods: Maple; oak; cherry
Number of parts: 16
Assembly time: 2 1/2
  hours
Price: $68.00 maple;
  $80.00 oak and cherry

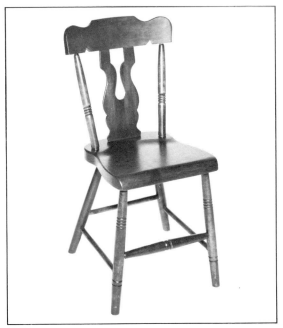

Kit: Fiddleback chair
Period: 1820–1860
Company: Zimmerman
  Chair Shop
Dimensions: 16″W x 15″D
  x 33″H
Woods: Maple; oak; cherry
Number of parts: 13
Assembly time: 2 hours
Price: $54.00 maple;
  $59.00 oak and cherry

*This chair, which originated
in Pennsylvania, features a
scrolled crest rail, ring-
turned legs, and a fiddleback splat, which is also
called a bootjack splat.*

COLONIAL KITS (1650–1800)

Kit: Duxbury desk chair
Period: Circa 1800
(adaptation with rollers)
Company: Zimmerman
Chair Shop
Dimensions: 20″W
x 17 1/2″D x 36″H
Woods: Maple; oak; cherry
Number of parts: 25
Assembly time: 3 hours
Price: $130.00 maple;
$145.00 oak and cherry

*This is a typical fanback
Windsor design, characterized by five to seven spindles and a saddle seat that
is usually shield-shaped.*

Kit: Country tavern bar
stool
Period: 1820s (Windsor
inspired)
Company: The Hardwood
Craftsman, Ltd.
Dimensions: 15 5/8″
diameter x 30″H (seat)
Wood: Birch
Number of parts: 16
Assembly time: 3 hours
Price: $109.00

Kit: Candle stand
Period: Eighteenth
century
Company: Cohassset
Colonials
Dimensions: 13″ top
diameter x 25″H
Wood: Maple
Number of parts: 5
Assembly time: 1 hour
Price: $28.00

*This is the solid maple can-
dle stand that got us off
and running with kits. It
has numerous uses and will
support a candlestick,
plant, or teacup beautifully.*

Kit: New England candle
stand
Period: Eighteenth
century
Company: The Western
Reserve Antique
Furniture Kit
Dimensions: 13″ diameter
x 26″H
Woods: Pine/maple/birch;
cherry; walnut
Number of parts: 5
Assembly time: 1 hour
Price: $27.95 ppd. pine/
maple/birch; $89.95 ppd.
cherry; $174.95 ppd.
walnut

Kit: Half-round table
Period: Seventeenth century
Company: Cohasset Colonials
Dimensions: 36″W x 18″D x 28 1/2″H
Woods: Pine/maple
Number of parts: 6
Assembly time: 1 hour
Price: $59.00

This half-round table is a perfect piece for a tight hallway or foyer. The pine top is knotless.

Kit: Joint stool
Period: Circa 1690
Company: The Bartley Collection, Ltd.
Dimensions: 20 3/4″W x 12 5/8″D x 18 3/4″H
Wood: Cherry
Number of parts: 9
Assembly time: 2–3 hours
Price: $150.00

Kit: Butterfly table
Period: Circa 1720
Company: The Bartley Collection, Ltd.
Dimensions: 24″ diameter (leaves up) x 21″H
Woods: Mahogany; cherry
Number of parts: 17
Assembly time: 3 hours
Price: $195.00 both woods

Kit: Butterfly table
Period: Eighteenth century
Company: Cohasset Colonials
Dimensions: 35 1/2″W x 29″D (leaves up) x 24 1/2″H
Wood: Maple
Number of parts: 21
Assembly time: 2 1/2–3 hours
Price: $127.00

The splayed, turned legs and swing-out leaf supports give this table the appearance of being supported by butterfly wings. Made in southern New England from 1700 to 1735, original butterfly tables are among the most rare and valued antiques today.

COLONIAL KITS (1650–1800)

Kit: Trestle table
Period: Circa 1650
Company: The Bartley Collection, Ltd.
Dimensions: 48"W x 35"D x 30"H; 60"W x 35"D x 30"H; 72"W x 35"D x 30"H
Wood: Ash
Number of parts: 18
Assembly time: 2–3 hours
Price: $402.00; $440.00; $474.00

A true trestle table is not permanently joined and can be disassembled and stored. Bartley's trestle, based on one from Plymouth, Massachusetts, is extremely simple to assemble, very durable, and can be taken apart for moving—just like the original ones.

Kit: Hunt table
Period: Eighteenth century
Company: Yield House
Dimensions: 55"W x 15"D x 28 3/4"H
Wood: Pine
Number of parts: 13
Assembly time: 1 1/2–2 hours
Price: $89.00

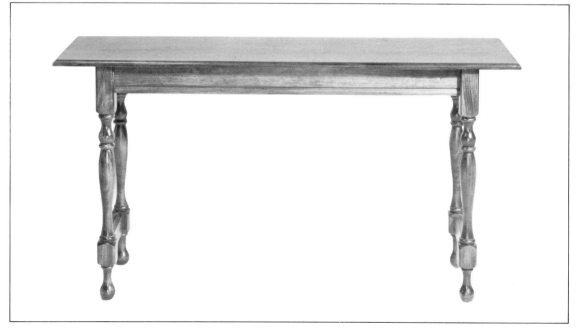

Kit: Writing table
Period: Eighteenth century
Company: Cohasset Colonials
Dimensions: 42″W x 26″D x 30″H
Wood: Maple
Number of parts: 17
Assembly time: 3 hours
Price: $189.00

Kit: Round table
Period: Eighteenth century
Company: Cohasset Colonials
Dimensions: 45″ top diameter x 30″H
Woods: Pine top; maple legs
Number of parts: 9
Assembly time: 2 hours
Price: $125.00

Kit: Footstool
Period: Eighteenth century
Company: The Western Reserve Antique Furniture Kit
Dimensions: 18″W x 7″D x 9″H
Wood: Pine
Number of parts: 5
Assembly time: 1 hour
Price: $19.95 ppd.

Kit: Howland water bench
Period: Seventeenth century
Company: Cohasset Colonials
Dimensions: 36 1/2″W x 12″D x 52″H
Wood: Pine
Number of parts: 6
Assembly time: 1 hour
Price: $123.00

Colonists used these shelves to hold their water buckets in the kitchen. Today this unit is perfect for storing books, records, or plants—or to use as a bar. The original is on display at the Jabez Howland House in Plymouth, Massachusetts.

COLONIAL KITS (1650–1800)

Kit: Four-shelf bookcase
Period: Early eighteenth century (adaptation)
Company: American Forest Products Company
Dimensions: 35″W x 12 3/4″D x 55 3/16″H
Wood: Pine
Number of parts: 25
Assembly time: 1 1/2 hours
Price: $99.95
Note: Also available in a three-shelf version (35″W x 10 11/16″D x 35 5/16″H) for $59.95

Kit: Rolltop desk
Period: Early American
Company: Yield House
Dimensions: 53 1/2″W x 27″D x 44″H
Wood: Pine
Number of parts: 146
Assembly time: 30–40 hours
Price: $579.00 ppd.
Note: Tambour rolltop is preassembled.

This pine desk has a number of fine accents, among them two deep filing drawers, a tambour roll that locks, and handsome carved bracket feet.

Kit: Drop-lid secretarial desk
Period: Early eighteenth century (adaptation)
Company: American Forest Products Company
Dimensions: 30 9/16″W x 15 5/8″D x 44 1/16″H
Wood: Pine
Number of parts: 51
Assembly time: 4 hours
Price: $164.95

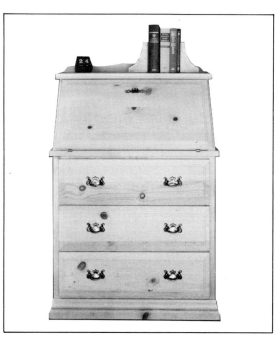

Kit: Rolltop desk
Period: Early American
Company: American Forest Products Company
Dimensions: 55″W x 22″D x 45 1/16″H
Wood: Pine
Number of parts: 104
Assembly time: 8–9 hours
Price: $259.95

Kit: Governor Winthrop
desk
Period: Eighteenth
century (adaptation)
Company: Yield House
Dimensions: 36"W x 18"D
x 39"H
Wood: Pine
Number of parts: 67
Assembly time: 5–6 hours
Price: $179.00 ppd.

Kit: Three-drawer file
cabinet
Period: Early American
Company: Yield House
Dimensions: 15 1/2"W
x 19"D x 38"H
Wood: Pine
Number of parts: 35
Assembly time: 2–3 hours
Price: $139.00 ppd.

Kit: Four-drawer chest
Period: Early eighteenth
century (adaptation)
Company: American
Forest Products
Company
Dimensions: 30 9/16"W
x 16 5/16"D x 39 1/16"H
Wood: Pine
Number of parts: 51
Assembly time: 4 hours
Price: $104.95

Kit: Map chest
Period: Eighteenth
century
Company: Yield House
Dimensions: 27"W
x 16 3/4"D x 24 1/2"H
Wood: Pine
Number of parts: 53; 2
preassembled frames
Assembly time: 3 1/2
hours
Price: $139.00

COLONIAL KITS (1650–1800)

Kit: Nightstand
Period: Early nineteenth century
Company: The Bartley Collection, Ltd.
Dimensions: 20″W x 16″D x 29″H
Woods: Cherry; mahogany
Number of parts: 17
Assembly time: 3 hours
Price: $295.00 both woods

This delicate nightstand is an adaptation of a nineteenth-century painted washstand.

Kit: Four-poster canopy bed
Period: Circa 1750
Company: Cohasset Colonials
Dimensions: (full size shown) 58″W x 80″L x 77″H
Woods: Pine/maple
Number of parts: 22
Assembly time: 1 1/2 hours
Price: $259.00

Our favorite kit, and the most attractive and well-built bed for the price you'll find anywhere—I guarantee it. You can order the fishnet canopy separately ($190 for a full size). The canopy bed is also available in twin and queen sizes.

Kit: Low bed with trundle
Period: Eighteenth century
Company: Cohasset Colonials
Dimensions: 59″W x 80″L x 33″H (bed); 34″W x 74 1/2″L x 9″H (trundle)
Woods: Pine/maple
Number of parts: 10 (bed); 13 (trundle)
Assembly time: 2 hours each
Price: $225.00 (full-size bed); $119.00 (trundle); $70.00 (foam rubber trundle mattress)

The original of this attractive low bed is in the Thomas Hart Room at the Metropolitan Museum of Art.

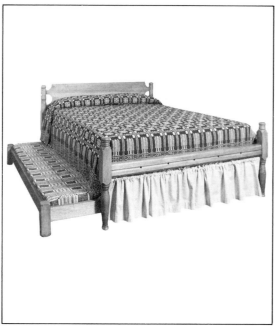

Kit: Armoire
Period: Early eighteenth century (adaptation)
Company: American Forest Products Company
Dimensions: 30 9/16″W x 16 5/16″D x 54 3/16″H
Wood: Pine
Number of parts: 73
Assembly time: 8–9 hours
Price: $164.95

Kit: Dover china cupboard
Period: Circa 1750 (Queen Anne influence)
Company: Outer Banks Pine Products
Dimensions: 37 5/8″W x 27 1/16″D x 88 1/2″H
Wood: Pine
Number of parts: 18
Assembly time: 3 hours
Price: $350.00

Raised panel doors, scalloped-edge shelves, and a finished back are among the distinctive features of this finely crafted cabinet. Note the classic bonnet top with the urn finial. The glass front is included in the kit.

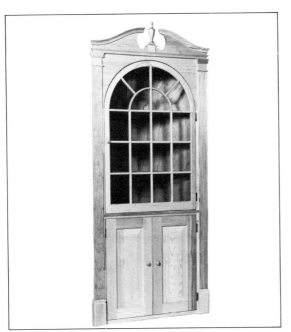

Kit: Salem corner cupboard
Period: Circa 1775
Company: Outer Banks Pine Products
Dimensions: 37 5/8″W x 27 1/16″D x 82″H
Wood: Pine
Number of parts: 19
Assembly time: 3 hours
Price: $350.00

Kit: Hutch
Period: Early eighteenth century
Company: American Forest Products Company
Dimensions: 28 11/16″W x 16 5/16″D x 71 7/8″H
Wood: Pine
Number of parts: 50
Assembly time: 4–5 hours
Price: $139.95

Kit: Corner cupboard
Period: Eighteenth century
Company: Yield House
Dimensions: 37 1/2″W x 16 3/4″D x 72″H
Wood: Pine
Number of parts: 40
Assembly time: 3–4 hours
Price: $279.00 ppd.

A model of understated beauty and practicality, this functional cupboard features deep display shelves, which are grooved to hold plates upright.

COLONIAL KITS (1650–1800)

Kit: Cubbyhole organizer
Period: Early American
Company: Yield House
Dimensions: 19 1/2"W
  x 6 1/4"D x 12"H
Wood: Pine
Number of parts: 25
Assembly time: 1 1/2
  hours
Price: $29.00

Kit: Cosmetic cabinet
Period: Early American
Company: Yield House
Dimensions: 18 3/4"W
  x 5 1/4"D x 28"H
Wood: Pine
Number of parts: 20
Assembly time: 2 hours
Price: $49.00

Although the louvered doors lend a more contemporary look, the design roots of this cabinet, with its scalloped top and scrolled sides, lie in the Colonial period.

Kit: Small shelves
Period: Eighteenth
  century
Company: The Western
  Reserve Antique
  Furniture Kit
Dimensions: 8"W x 6"D
  x 18"H
Woods: Pine; cherry;
  walnut
Number of parts: 4
Assembly time: 1/2 hour
Price: $24.95 ppd. pine;
  $44.95 ppd. cherry;
  $79.95 ppd. walnut

Kit: Fishtail pipe box
Period: 1800s
Company: Cohasset
  Colonials
Dimensions: 5 3/4"W
  x 3 1/2"D x 19 1/2"H
Woods: Pine/maple
Number of parts: 12
Assembly time: 1 1/2
  hours
Price: $34.00

During colonial times, pipe boxes like these were a permanent fixture near the fireplace and held the long-stem, communal pipes and the tobacco. People today use these handy boxes to hold candles, paintbrushes, or knitting needles.

Kit: Tapered pipe box
Period: Eighteenth century
Company: The Western Reserve Antique Furniture Kit
Dimensions: 6″W x 4″D x 19″H
Woods: Pine/poplar; cherry; walnut
Number of parts: 11
Assembly time: 1 1/2 hours
Price: $39.95 ppd. pine/poplar; $89.95 ppd. cherry; $109.95 ppd. walnut

Kit: Wall sconce
Period: Eighteenth century
Company: The Western Reserve Antique Furniture Kit
Dimensions: 9″W x 5″D x 14″H
Wood: Pine
Number of parts: 4
Assembly time: 20 minutes
Price: $14.95 ppd.

Kit: Wall box
Period: Eighteenth century
Company: The Western Reserve Antique Furniture Kit
Dimensions: 11″W x 5″D x 9″H
Wood: Pine
Number of parts: 5
Assembly time: 1/2 hour
Price: $19.95 ppd.

Kit: Pennsylvania Dutch wall box
Period: Eighteenth century
Company: The Western Reserve Antique Furniture Kit
Dimensions: 12″W x 4″D x 14″H
Wood: Pine
Number of parts: 7
Assembly time: 1 hour
Price: $35.95 ppd.

The original of this box was painted (as were most Pennsylvania Dutch furnishings). Note the graceful cyma curves on the front, a favorite design motif typical of Queen Anne pieces.

COLONIAL KITS (1650–1800)

Kit: Cranberry scoop
Period: 1800s
Company: The Western Reserve Antique Furniture Kit
Dimensions: 8″W x 3″D x 8″H
Wood: Pine
Number of parts: 6
Assembly time: 1 hour
Price: $19.95 ppd.

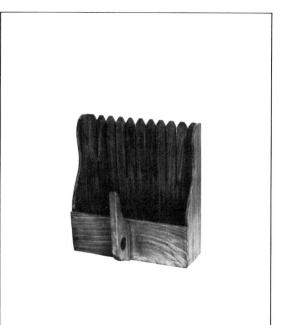

Kit: Tray
Period: Eighteenth century
Company: The Western Reserve Antique Furniture Kit
Dimensions: 24″W x 12″D
Woods: Pine; cherry; walnut
Number of parts: 7
Assembly time: 1 hour
Price: $24.95 ppd. pine; $44.95 ppd. cherry; $74.95 ppd. walnut

Kit: Courting mirror
Period: Eighteenth century
Company: Cohasset Colonials
Dimensions: 9 5/8″W x 12 1/4″H
Wood: Pine
Number of parts: 6
Assembly time: 1/2 hour
Price: $24.00
Note: Glass is single-shock silvered, giving it an uneven handblown look.

Because glass during colonial times was just as valuable as diamonds, a man who was serious about a certain woman often gave her a courting mirror as a token of his affection.

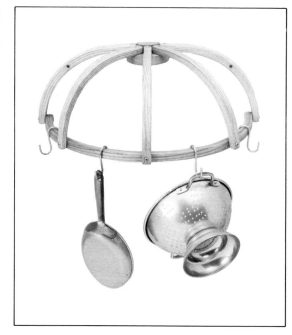

Kit: Pot and plant holder
Period: Country
Company: Woodcraft Supply Corp.
Dimensions: 21″W x 12″D x 10 1/2″H
Wood: White ash
Number of parts: 7
Assembly time: 30 minutes
Price: $42.25 ppd.

Clearly not a Colonial item in the strict sense, this pot rack is marvelous nonetheless for accessorizing today's popular country look. Handy for displaying plants and mugs, too.

Kit: Rocking horse
Period: Nineteenth century
Company: Woodcraft Supply Corp.
Dimensions: 48″L x 20″H (back)
Wood: Sugar pine
Number of parts: 16
Assembly time: 2–3 hours assembly; 20–30 hours carving
Price: $104.95 ppd.

With an additional investment of about $25 for a basic set of carving tools, even novice woodcarvers can successfully complete this project, provided they carefully follow the detailed instructions in the accompanying book.

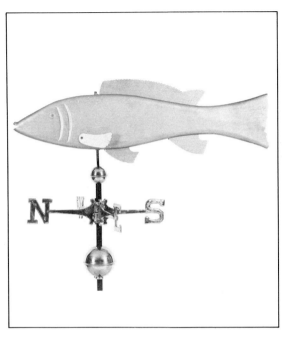

Kit: Codfish weathervane
Period: Eighteenth century
Company: Cohasset Colonials
Dimensions: 32″W x 10″H
Wood: Pine
Number of parts: 6
Assembly time: 1 hour
Price: $85.00 including weathervane hardware
Note: Fish can be purchased separately for $45.00 without hardware.

Kit: Martha Ann quilt rack
Period: Early American
Company: Yield House
Dimensions: 23 1/2″W x 15 1/2″D x 30″H
Wood: Pine
Number of parts: 6
Assembly time: 15 minutes
Price: $34.00

No glue is required to assemble this rack; you just tighten the nuts and you have a towel or quilt rack in minutes. An exceptionally fine design at a low price.

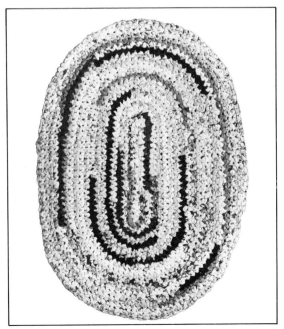

Kit: Colonial rag rug
Period: Eighteenth century
Company: Country Rag Rugs
Dimensions: 2′ x 3′
Materials: Handmade maple crochet hook, 3 3/4 pounds of cotton-blend strips
Number of parts: Hook, rags, direction book, and tote bag
Assembly time: 10–12 hours
Price: $25.00

COLONIAL KITS (1650—1800)

Kit: Lift-top commode
Period: Early nineteenth century
Company: Fred Ellis & Sons, Inc.
Dimensions: 30″W x 15″D x 29″H
Wood: Pine
Number of parts: 30
Assembly time: 4 hours
Price: $155.00

Kit: Sea chest
Period: Early nineteenth century
Company: Fred Ellis & Sons, Inc.
Dimensions: 35″W x 16″D x 15″H
Wood: Pine
Number of parts: 8
Assembly time: 1 1/2 hours
Price: $150.00

Kit: Small six-board chest
Period: Eighteenth century
Company: The Western Reserve Antique Furniture Kit
Dimensions: 20″W x 9″D x 15″H
Wood: Pine
Number of parts: 6
Assembly time: 1 hour
Price: $34.95 ppd.

Kit: Shaker hanging
   cupboard
Period: Early 1800s
Company: Yield House
Dimensions: 19"W
   x 8 1/4"D x 25 1/2"H
Wood: Pine
Number of parts: 8
Assembly time: 1 1/2
   hours
Price: $49.00

*This pine cupboard, a fa-
vorite of ours, makes a
dandy spice cabinet in the
kitchen or a medicine chest
in the bathroom.*

SHAKER KITS (1780–1860)

Austere, functional, ascetic. All of these adjectives have been used to describe the Shakers, a 200-year-old religious sect known for its celibate lifestyle, its ingenious inventions (the clothespin and flat broom among them), and the simple lines and practical beauty of its furniture design.

Originally called Shaking Quakers because of their habit of shaking and whirling during religious worship, the Shakers settled in America in 1774 under the leadership of Mother Ann Lee and went on to establish a unique communal order.

Above all, three fundamental doctrines guided their lives: purity, community, and simplicity. In their pursuit of an inner spiritual order, the Shakers rejected worldly desires and ornamentation in their surroundings.

Because even the objects they crafted bore the stamp of a communal effort, Shaker products tended to look the same. But their standards of excellence were so high, and the shared pool of talent and ideas so rich, that "mass" production under the Shaker furniture-makers reached unprecedented heights.

Eschewing the cabriole legs and splat chair backs so popular at the time, Shaker cabinetmakers cleanly tapered their table and desk legs and often crafted chairs with low backs that could be easily slid under the table and out of the way. With comfort as well as usefulness in mind, they added wood ball-and-socket devices to the bottom of back chair legs, thus permitting the occupant to tilt backward without scraping the floor.

The Shakers' sense of orderliness was nowhere more apparent than in their living spaces. Walls of houses and shops were lined with floor-to-ceiling cupboards, in which everything had its place, from clothing to medicinal herbs. Beds folded up flat against the wall when not in use, forming a hutch seat with storage space. Desks, laundry tables, and sewing tables were long and designed with drawers that could move from one side to the other to accommodate two people working at the same time. From pegboards fastened to the wall, usually 6 feet above the floor, hung bonnets, dried herbs and flowers, chairs, and clocks. Shakers used pine stools with two, three, and even four steps to reach these high places.

Because Shakers favored white, or soft, pine for their cupboards and benches, they owned large tracts of woodland adjacent to their societies. One distinctive feature of Shaker pine furniture is the disclosure of the edge, or end, grain, which was made possible by cutting the wood radially. This method also eliminated warping in large, flat surfaces. Rock, or sugar, maple was used to fashion table legs and chair posts. Shaker craftspeople (both Sisters and Brothers engaged in cabinetmaking) also used black cherry, yellow birch, basswood, beech, and butternut for certain pieces.

The chair, available in some 50 sizes and models, was one of the few cash crops made by the Shakers and sold to the outside world. In the 1870s, chairs made by one Shaker society were sold at Macy's in New York and Marshall Field's in Chicago.

Most chairs had woven tapes for seats, either in contrasting colors or in stripes; many had mushroom-cap turnings on armrests and ball-and-socket tilting devices on back legs. Early examples of Shaker chairs were often stained a fairly colorful ocher.

It may seem inconsistent that the Shakers used color as freely as they did. Yet color can be observed in their weavings, herb and seed labels, bookbindings, boxes, and spool stands. An indigo-based blue, red shades, and yellow, especially mustard, were the most common. The terms *Shaker red* and *Shaker blue* are actually misnomers, since Shaker shades were not uniform—yellows varied from pale to bright canary, and reds from terra cotta to coral to bright "Chinese" red on some painted banisters.

Early Shaker cabinetmakers usually gave furniture a coat of paint to preserve the wood but later began to thin the paint or to use a stain so that the texture and grain pattern of the wood were apparent. They also applied oils and earth-tone water paints or stains, which gave pieces a cinnamon or tawny brown color. Although varnish was employed, an 1845 law declared that it could be applied only to movable items in dwellings such as tables and bureaus, but never to stationary cabinets or ceilings. It is thought that the Shakers rubbed pieces of salt pork onto their furniture to produce a nontoxic natural oil finish that did not become rancid.

In the mid-1860s, the Eldress at the Central Ministry in Canterbury, New Hampshire, had a painful decision to make—either admit new members and keep Shakerism alive or close the doors of the community. She decided to close membership and thus spelled the end of the longest-lived communal religious society in American history. Today only

The Shaker tree of life.

SHAKER KITS (1780–1860)

a few Shakers remain in two of the original 19 societies: Canterbury, New Hampshire and Sabbathday Lake, Maine. But "with hands to work and hearts to God," Shakers still grow and sell herbs, vinegars, and potpourri by mail and in their shop at Sabbathday Lake. For information and a catalog, write the United Society of Shakers, Sabbathday Lake, ME 04724.

Shaker designs were among the first to be reproduced by kit makers. The simple, clean lines and joinery lend themselves beautifully to production in unassembled form.

When Francis Hagerty, late founder of Cohasset Colonials in Cohasset, Massachusetts, offered his first line of kits for sale by mail in 1950, many of his original 15 kits were Shaker inspired. For the next 20 years, Cohasset all but dominated the Shaker kit market. It wasn't until 1971, when Shaker Workshops set up shop in Concord, Massachusetts, that a kit company existed to produce Shaker kits exclusively. Within the past few years, Yield House, in North Conway, New Hampshire, and Western Reserve Antique Furniture Kit, in Bath, Ohio, have both initiated lines of Shaker kits.

Of the six or so companies producing Shaker kits today, these four are, from my personal experience, the most reliable and carry the widest range of Shaker items. The prototypes for the pieces manufactured by Cohasset, Shaker Workshops, and Western Reserve are based on specific Shaker items housed today in museums and private collections, such as Hancock Shaker Village (Hancock, Massachusetts), the Shaker Museum (Old Chatham, New York), and the Shaker Historical Society (Shaker Heights, Ohio—former site of the North Union Shaker Community, now defunct). As of this writing, Shaker Workshops is the exclusive supplier of chairs to the Central Ministry in Canterbury.

All four of the above companies are represented in the following section. You'll notice in thumbing through the pages that Yield House's kits are consistently lower in price than the others. All Shaker kits from Yield House are constructed of northern pine, a softer and less expensive wood than maple, cherry, or walnut.

Western Reserve and Yield House sell kits in both assembled and unassembled form. Assembly fees at Western Reserve run anywhere from $15.00 for the $19.95 pine cranberry scoop to $175.00 for the $134.95 drop-leaf table.

Yield House's finished pieces cost only 25 percent more than their unfinished ones, but although they are finished adequately, the quality cannot match the hand-rubbed waxed patina of Western Reserve's pieces. You pay for the difference, however.

All companies include seat tapes as a standard item with their chair kits; Western Reserve and Cohasset will, if you specify, send a rushing kit as an alternative. I think that seat tapes are more attractive, far easier, and faster to weave than rushing and more Shaker in character since the Shakers usually taped their chairs. Shaker Workshops offers the widest variety in colors (even stripes) and widths of tapes. With the exception of Yield House, all Shaker kit manufacturers include a small container of stain with each kit. The stains vary to some extent, but all are in the medium-brown range.

Once you've completed a Shaker kit, I think you'll find it will blend in wonderfully with a wide variety of furnishings, from butcher block to Queen Anne. We have several Queen Anne kit pieces in our living room along with one large Shaker table, and they all co-exist, filling the space with their own distinctive measure of quiet dignity. I think the Shakers would approve.

Kit: Shaker side chair
Period: Early 1800s
Company: Cohasset Colonials
Dimensions: 19"W x 15"D x 41"H
Wood: Maple
Number of parts: 18
Assembly time: 5–6 hours including seat weaving
Price: $87.00
Note: Chair tapes are available in black and cocoa only.

Note the inventive Shaker tilting device on the bottoms of the back legs. This ball-and-socket facilitates leaning back in the chair and also protects floor surfaces from scratches.

Kit: Straight chair
Period: Early 1800s
Company: Shaker Workshops
Dimensions: 18 3/4"W x 14"D x 42"H
Wood: Maple
Number of parts: 18
Assembly time: 5–6 hours including seat weaving
Price: $65.00
Note: Chair tapes are available in 15 colors, including stripes.

SHAKER KITS (1780–1860)

Kit: Shaker side chair
Period: Early 1800s
Company: Cohasset
Colonials
Dimensions: 19″W x 15″D
x 41″H
Wood: Maple
Number of parts: 18
Assembly time: 5–6 hours
including seat rushing
Price: $69.00

Kit: Elder's chair
Period: Early 1800s
Company: Shaker
Workshops
Dimensions: 22″W x 18″D
x 51 1/2″H
Wood: Maple
Number of parts: 24
Assembly time: 5–6 hours
including seat weaving
Price: $110.00
Note: Chair tapes are
available in 15 colors,
including stripes.

Kit: Shawl-back rocker
Period: Mid–1800s
Company: Shaker
Workshops
Dimensions: 23″W x 19″D
x 42″H
Wood: Maple
Number of parts: 26
Assembly time: 5–6 hours
including seat weaving
Price: $125.00
Note: Chair tapes are
available in 15 colors,
including stripes.

Kit: Tape-back rocker
Period: Mid–1800s
Company: Shaker
Workshops
Dimensions: 23″W x 19″D
x 42″H
Wood: Maple
Number of parts: 24
Assembly time: 5–6 hours
including seat weaving
Price: $130.00
Note: Chair tapes are
available in 15 colors,
including stripes.

This rocker closely resembles one produced by the Shakers at the Mount Lebanon, New York, community during the nineteenth century. The turnings on the arm rests are called mushroom caps, a Shaker design innovation.

Kit: Shaker settee
Period: Shaker
Company: Shaker Workshops
Dimensions: 43 1/4″W x19″D x 37 1/2″H
Wood: Rock maple
Number of parts: 23
Assembly time: 8 hours
Price: $200.00
Note: Seat tapes are available in 15 colors, including stripes.

This elegant settee was originally made toward the end of the nineteenth century in the South Family chair shop at Mount Lebanon, New York. Very few have survived.

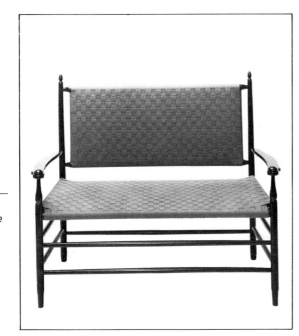

Kit: Shaker low-back dining chair
Period: Early 1800s
Company: The Western Reserve Antique Furniture Kit
Dimensions: 19″W x 15″D x 26″H
Woods: Maple/birch
Number of parts: 12
Assembly time: 4–5 hours including seat weaving
Price: $89.95 ppd.

This low-back chair, which served as a model for the modern Danish dining chair, was designed so that it could be pushed under the table after eating to clear the way for cleaning.

Kit: Weaver's chair
Period: Early 1800s
Company: Shaker Workshops
Dimensions: 18 3/4″W x 14″D x 26″H (seat); 39″H
Wood: Maple
Number of parts: 16
Assembly time: 4–5 hours including seat weaving
Price: $62.50
Note: Chair tapes are available in 15 colors, including stripes.

The weaver's chair is ideally suited for use as a bar or counter chair. Shakers used them to sit at their looms, the high seat enabling them to lean closer to their work.

Kit: Low-back chair
Period: Early 1800s
Company: Shaker Workshops
Dimensions: 18 3/4″W x 14″D x 27″H
Wood: Maple
Number of parts: 17
Assembly time: 4–5 hours including seat weaving
Price: $55.00
Note: Chair tapes are available in 15 colors, including stripes.

SHAKER KITS (1780–1860)

Kit: Child's rocker (ages 3–7)
Period: Mid–1800s
Company: Shaker Workshops
Dimensions: 15″W x 11 1/2″D x 29″H
Wood: Maple
Number of parts: 24
Assembly time: 4–5 hours including seat weaving
Price: $60.00
Note: Chair tapes are available in 15 colors, including stripes.

Kit: Shaker bench
Period: Early 1800s
Company: The Western Reserve Antique Furniture Kit
Dimensions: 36″W x 10″D x 17″H
Woods: Pine; cherry; walnut
Number of parts: 7
Assembly time: 1 1/2 hours
Price: $34.95 ppd. pine; $74.95 ppd. cherry; $109.95 ppd. walnut

Kit: Shaker stool
Period: Early 1800s
Company: The Western Reserve Antique Furniture Kit
Dimensions: 17″W x 9″D x 15″H
Woods: Pine; cherry; walnut
Number of parts: 6
Assembly time: 1 hour
Price: $25.95 ppd. pine; $64.95 ppd. cherry; $94.95 ppd. walnut

Dado joints and cross-bracing on this stool make it a very durable piece. In addition to being useful to sit on, the Shaker stool makes a terrific portable table—or a spot to show off your plant collection.

Kit: Spinning stool
Period: Mid–1800s
Company: Shaker Workshops
Dimensions: 18″W x 14″D x 15 1/2″H
Wood: Maple
Number of parts: 16
Assembly time: 3 hours including seat weaving
Price: $37.50
Note: Seat tapes are available in 15 colors, including stripes.

Kit: Footstool
Period: Mid–1800s
Company: Shaker
Workshops
Dimensions: 13″W x 10″D
x 10″H
Wood: Maple
Number of parts: 12
Assembly time: 2 1/2
hours including seat
weaving
Price: $27.50
Note: Seat tapes are
available in 15 colors,
including stripes.

This footstool makes a perfect companion for any of the Shaker rockers. It's sturdy enough, too, to serve as a stool for a youngster.

Kit: Shaker step stool
Period: 1800s
Company: Cohasset
Colonials
Dimensions: 7 1/2″W
x 13″D x 33″H; step 9″H
Wood: Pine
Number of parts: 4
Assembly time: 1 hour
Price: $35.00

Shakers used step stools like this one to reach their high, built-in drawers and closets. Tuck it into a corner when not in use or hang it from a peg on the wall— as they did.

Kit: Shaker table
Period: Circa 1800
Company: Cohasset
Colonials
Dimensions: 17 3/4″ top
diameter x 25″H
Wood: Maple
Number of parts: 7
Assembly time: 1 hour
Price: $42.00
Note: A similar table is
available from Shaker
Workshops for $45.00.

Used to furnish the retiring rooms of Shaker communal dwellings, these graceful tables work equally well today in the hallway, the bedroom, or the living room, next to a Shaker rocker.

Kit: Rectangular candle
stand
Period: Early 1800s
Company: Shaker
Workshops
Dimensions: 20″W
x 17 3/4″D x 25 1/2″H
Wood: Maple
Number of parts: 6
Assembly time: 1 hour
Price: $45.00

SHAKER KITS (1780–1860)

Kit: Shaker tray
Period: Circa 1800
Company: Cohasset
Colonials
Dimensions: 30″W
x 18 1/2″D x 36″H
Wood: Pine
Number of parts: 16
Assembly time: 1 1/2–2
hours
Price: $75.00

Kit: Night table
Period: Eighteenth
century
Company: Cohasset
Colonials
Dimensions: 18 1/2″W
x 18 1/2″D x 28 1/2″H
Woods: Pine/maple
Number of parts: 14
Assembly time: 2 hours
Price: $89.00

*Modeled after an original
piece now housed in the
Pierce Hitchborn House in
Boston, this Shaker table,
with its elegant, clean lines,
is suitable as a night table
in the bedroom or as a telephone stand.*

Kit: Shaker trestle table
Period: 1840s
Company: The Western
Reserve Antique
Furniture Kit
Dimensions: 29″W x 18″D
x 28″H
Woods: Pine/maple/birch;
cherry; walnut
Number of parts: 8
Assembly time: 1 1/2–2
hours
Price: $109.95 ppd.
pine/maple/birch;
$179.95 ppd. cherry;
$299.95 ppd. walnut
Note: Leg units are
preassembled.

*This delicately shaped tres-
tle table, actually a smaller
version of a dining table,
makes a perfect writing
area or a cozy table for two.*

Kit: Shaker drop-leaf table
Period: Early 1800s
Company: The Western
Reserve Antique
Furniture Kit
Dimensions: 36″W x 25″D
(leaf up) x 27″H
Woods: Pine/maple/birch;
cherry; walnut
Number of parts: 11
Assembly time: 3–4 hours
Price: $134.95 ppd.
pine/maple/birch;
$209.95 ppd. cherry;
$374.95 ppd. walnut
Note: Front and back leg
units are preassembled.

Kit: Harvest table
Period: Eighteenth century
Company: Cohasset Colonials
Dimensions: 72″W x 42″D (leaves up) x 30″H
Woods: Pine/maple
Number of parts: 9
Assembly time: 4 hours
Price: $265.00

Cohasset is the only kit company I know of to offer this magnificent harvest table. It seats eight comfortably and is ideal for a narrow dining room. When not using ours, we place it behind the couch in front of the windows and use it to display plants and old crockery.

Kit: Large Shaker dining table
Period: Circa 1800
Company: Cohasset Colonials
Dimensions: 82″W x 30″D x 30″H
Wood: Pine
Number of parts: 9
Assembly time: 2 hours
Price: $239.00

Chamfered (beveled) pine legs and arched shoes highlight this sturdy table, which seats eight. (It is also available in a smaller version 54 inches long, seating four for $188.00.)

SHAKER KITS (1780–1860)

Kit: Shaker sewing chest
Period: Early 1800s
Company: Yield House
Dimensions: 20″W
 x 11 3/8″D x 24″H;
 drawers 2 1/4″H
Wood: Pine
Number of parts: 35
Assembly time: 5 hours
Price: $79.00
Note: Top lifts to reveal a
 compartment 4 7/8″D

The top of this handy little chest lifts to reveal a large compartment nearly 5 inches high. In addition to housing sewing supplies, it can also be stocked with linens or even serve as a lingerie chest in the bedroom.

Kit: Shaker six-board chest
Period: Early 1800s
Company: The Western
 Reserve Antique
 Furniture Kit
Dimensions: 38″W x 16″D
 x 18″H
Woods: Pine; cherry;
 walnut
Number of parts: 14
Assembly time: 2 1/2
 hours
Price: $104.95 ppd. pine;
 $224.95 ppd. cherry;
 $349.95 ppd. walnut

Called a blanket box by the Shakers, this piece has innumerable uses, with its roomy 3-foot-long interior. Note the fancy scrollwork on the legs, which are molded into ogee curves.

Kit: Shaker jelly cupboard
Period: Early 1800s
Company: Yield House
Dimensions: 22″W
 x 12 1/2″D x 51 3/4″H
Wood: Pine
Number of parts: 20
Assembly time: 3 hours
Price: $139.00 ppd.

Kit: Towel rack
Period: 1800s
Company: Shaker
 Workshops
Dimensions: 33 7/8″W
 x 33 1/2″H; foot 13″D
Wood: Pine
Number of parts: 8
Assembly time: 1 hour
Price: $35.00

Shakers made wide use of these movable racks in their kitchens and washhouses. Today they are useful for airing quilts or as a place to hang towels or wet clothing.

Kit: Shaker wall rack
Period: 1800s
Company: Cohasset Colonials
Dimensions: 27"W x 7 1/2"D x 25"H
Wood: Pine
Number of parts: 5 parts not including thongs
Assembly time: 1 hour
Price: $47.00

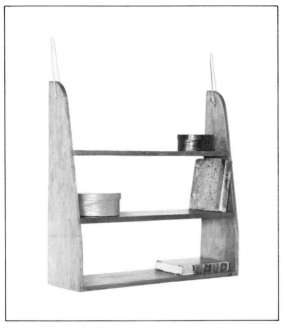

Kit: Shaker double candle sconce
Period: Circa 1800
Company: The Western Reserve Antique Furniture Kit
Dimensions: 11"W x 6"D x 19"H
Woods: Pine; cherry; walnut
Number of parts: 2
Assembly time: 20 minutes
Price: $19.50 ppd. pine; $24.95 ppd. cherry; $39.95 ppd. walnut

Shakers needed a maximum of light in their workrooms, so they designed this sconce, which holds two candles and rests on a shelf or hangs from a peg.

Kit: Shaker sconce
Period: 1800s
Company: Cohasset Colonials
Dimensions: 9"W x 6"D x 18"H
Wood: Pine
Number of parts: 5, tin candleholder included
Assembly time: 1/2 hour
Price: $29.00

This single pine sconce, based on one from a Shaker dwelling in Canterbury, New Hampshire, comes with its own tin candle-holder.

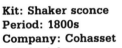

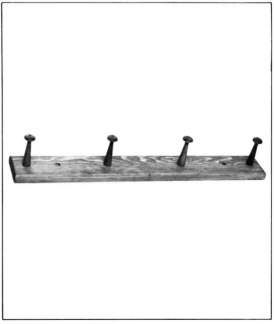

Kit: Shaker pegboard
Period: Circa 1800
Company: The Western Reserve Antique Furniture Kit
Dimensions: 24"W x 3"H; 36"W x 3"H
Woods: Pine/birch
Number of parts: 7; 9
Assembly time: 20 minutes
Price: $9.95 ppd.; $12.95 ppd.

These pegboards served as the focal point of the Shakers' ingenious organizational system. We use them in our small Vermont cabin (where floorspace is precious) to hang tools, clothing, and chairs.

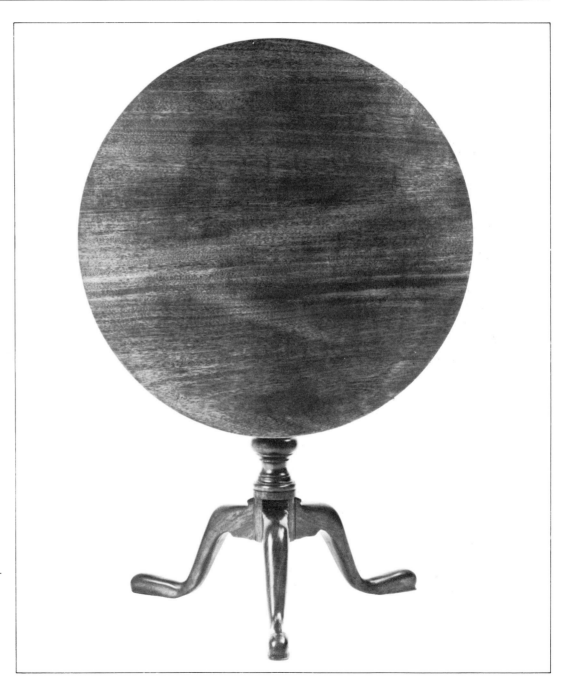

Kit: Tilt-top table
Period: 1740–1760, Queen Anne
Company: The Bartley Collection, Ltd.
Dimensions: 31″ top diameter x 28 1/2″H
Woods: Cherry; mahogany
Number of parts: 13
Assembly time: 3 hours
Price: $325.00 both woods

The top of this unusual table can be both revolved and tilted. Not visible is the so-called birdcage construction that permits this dual action. Note the characteristic snake feet.

QUEEN ANNE & CHIPPENDALE KITS (1720–1795)

The Queen Anne period lasted in England for about 40 years (1702 to 1745), beginning with the reign of Queen Anne and extending through the reign of George I. The Queen Anne style caught on in the colonies around 1720, coinciding with an improvement in living conditions, especially for urban residents. Representing a distinct departure from the stiff, rectangular, formal lines of the previous William and Mary period, Queen Anne furnishings are characterized by graceful curved lines, giving them a look of unmatched elegance. Three design features typify the period: the cabriole leg with its sweeping, reverse S-curve (sometimes called a cyma curve); club, or pad, feet and later in the period, claw-and-ball feet; and finally, the increasing use of mahogany in addition to the already popular walnut. Other significant details include carved shell and fan designs and solid splats and rounded shoulders on chair backs.

Full adoption of the Queen Anne style resulted in the crafting of many fine chairs, highboys and lowboys, the finest examples of which bring upwards of $20,000 at prestige auction houses today. At present, quality American Queen Anne furniture is more highly prized by American collectors of antiques than its English counterpart.

Although utilitarian pine furniture continued to be produced in the colonies, especially in rural areas, furniture styles began to advance in design and construction in response to the increasing number of people of means living in cities such as New York and Philadelphia.

Fine woods were brought from all over the world (until then choice hardwoods such as mahogany were virtually unavailable in the New World) and furniture proportions dramatically increased as room dimensions expanded. Rolltop desks, tea tables, lowboys and highboys, Pembroke tables, breakfronts, and China cabinets were in great demand. Different schools of cabinetry sprang up around large metropolitan centers, giving rise to such pieces as the Philadelphia highboy and the Connecticut, Boston, and Newport block-front chest.

Two of the most interesting elements employed in Queen Anne furniture were the cyma curve and, later, claw-and-ball feet. The painter and engraver Hogarth (1697–1764), called the cyma curve "the line of beauty" and drew such a shape in one of his paintings. Actually a continuous double curve, one part convex and the other concave, the cyma curve is especially noticeable in the designs of chair backs and cabriole legs. Two curves end to end form the scroll top on highboys and secretaries; two opposite each other form the outline of chair splats, a shape often likened to the contours of a Chinese vase.

The origin of the famous claw-and-ball foot is also Oriental—a dragon's triple claw grasping a sacred jewel. English cabinetmakers translated the dragon's paw into a bird's talon and used it to end the graceful cabriole leg of a chair, table, or bureau. In the colonies, the way the foot was carved varied enough from one cabinetmaker to the next that it became the signature of where the furniture was made and sometimes by whom.

One of the most formidable pieces of Queen Anne furniture is the highboy, which developed from a chest of drawers placed on a stand high enough that the lower drawers could be opened without stooping over. First imported from England during the latter part of the seventeenth century, highboys were copied by Colonial cabinetmakers, and later pieces, especially those made in Philadelphia, showed a distinctly American style. They evolved from the flattop style with six joined legs popular during the William and Mary period, to a four-legged cabriole style with carving, to a fussier highboy with a scroll-top, to the pièce de résistance, a lavish Philadelphia highboy in full Chippendale style, with claw-and-ball feet and elaborately carved ornaments, called cartouches, such as Cupids.

As Queen Anne evolved into Chippendale, ornament became more elaborate, reaching its apex under the skillful hand of the master carver, Thomas Chippendale. The Chippendale era marked the first time an English style was named for the cabinetmaker who originated it instead of for the reigning royal family. Chippendale, adopted in the colonies around 1755, continued in vogue until about 1790.

Fine chairs in the Chippendale style in the colonies were made exclusively of mahogany because it was an easier wood to carve. Top rails of chairs featured lavish Cupid's bow shapes, and carved shells decorated rail tops and appeared at the head of cabriole and straight legs, both of which were used in Chippendale pieces. In contrast to Queen Anne chairs, which usually featured a solid splat, Chippendale chairs were broad, square in shape, with a pierced slat.

QUEEN ANNE & CHIPPENDALE KITS (1720–1795)

Some furniture experts believe that American cabinetmakers produced better Chippendale than the master himself—especially John Goddard, a noted Rhode Island craftsman. One of Goddard's triumphs was to design what is probably the most elegant Chippendale-style piece created—the blockfront chest. Since no European prototype of this piece exists, it is thought to be a purely American phenomenon. This crowning achievement of the period is one that kit enthusiasts can own themselves, since one of these chests is available in unassembled form from The Bartley Collection.

Bartley's blockfront chest—not unlike Goddard's in design—was photographed for one of the step-by-step sections in the book (see pages 147–52). Although more difficult to assemble and more time-consuming to finish properly, a Queen Anne or Chippendale kit will bring years of satisfaction. These kits feature the same details and superb craftsmanship of the original pieces—table legs are dovetailed into pedestals, joints in chests are mortise-and-tenoned for utmost strength, drawers are dovetailed, and carved motifs and hardware are authentically reproduced.

The Bartley Collection was the first major kit company to offer Queen Anne and Chippendale designs for sale in unassembled form. Founded in 1974, in Prairie View, Illinois, by Kenneth Bartley Boudrie, Bartley led off its line with seven kits and has added from three to four new styles each subsequent year. As the exclusive manufacturer of a number of fine antique pieces from the Henry Ford Museum in Dearborn, Michigan, Bartley prides itself on producing high-quality furniture for customers who enjoy working with fine woods and appreciate superb joinery and detail.

Precut pieces (often in a choice of cherry or mahogany), glue, hardware—everything is included in kits sold by Bartley. If you prefer, the company will deliver already assembled, finished pieces at prices usually two to three times higher than in kit form.

Yield House, an old hand at producing Colonial kits of a more rustic style, has recently introduced a line of Queen Anne kits. Like its other unassembled pieces, its Queen Anne kits are constructed exclusively in northern pine and so are, compared to Bartley, considerably lower in price. Lowboys in the colonies were never built in pine—always walnut, maple, or cherry—and a lowboy in pine is not as elegant because the grain of pine always remains prominent and will not take a finish as finely as hardwoods. But the price is certainly affordable.

Emperor Clock Company, based in Fairhope, Alabama, also sells a less expensive selection of Queen Anne-inspired kits. Constructed in cherry, the line does not feature carved details, solid brass hardware, or refinements of construction—but again, prices are extremely reasonable.

Hardwood Craftsman, a new company on the kit scene, offers Queen Anne elegance at prices lower than Bartley, but higher than Yield House. All its kits are fashioned in cherry, birch, or oak. Hardwood Craftsman is able to cut costs by prefitting joints instead of dovetailing, by eliminating stain and finishing supplies, and by keeping decorative details to a minimum.

Whatever kit you decide to tackle, and from whichever company, I think you'll benefit greatly from an adventure with kits from this popular period in American furniture history.

Kit: Bench/footstool
Period: 1710, Queen Anne
Company: The Bartley Collection, Ltd.
Dimensions: 18 3/4"W x 15 1/2"D x 17 1/2"H
Woods: Cherry; mahogany
Number of parts: 13
Assembly time: 2 1/2 hours
Price: $210.00 both woods
Note: Upholstery fabric not included.

Fashioned in typical Queen Anne design, this stool functions superbly as a vanity stool or as a footstool to a wing chair. The upholstered top is a good spot to display a favorite needlepoint design.

Kit: Bench/footstool
Period: 1780, Chippendale
Company: The Bartley Collection, Ltd.
Dimensions: 18"W x 13"D x 17"H
Woods: Cherry; mahogany
Number of parts: 16
Assembly time: 2–3 hours
Price: $145.00 (both woods)

QUEEN ANNE & CHIPPENDALE KITS (1720–1795)

Kit: Side chair
Period: 1730, Queen Anne
Company: The Bartley
  Collection, Ltd.
Dimensions: 22″W
  x 21 1/2″D x 40″H
Woods: Cherry; mahogany
Number of parts: 10
Assembly time: 5–6 hours
Price: $306.00 both woods
Note: Upholstery fabric
  not included.

This typical example of an early Queen Anne chair has all the distinctive earmarks of the period: Chinese vase contours on the solid splat, rounded club feet, cabriole legs, and rounded shoulders.

Kit: Armchair
Period: 1730, Queen Anne
Company: The Bartley
  Collection, Ltd.
Dimensions: 26 1/2″W
  x 22 1/2″D x 40″H
Woods: Cherry; mahogany
Number of parts: 14
Assembly time: 6 hours
Price: $319.00 both woods
Note: Upholstery fabric
  not included.

Kit: Side chair
Period: 1740, Chippendale
Company: The Bartley
  Collection, Ltd.
Dimensions: 20″W
  x 21 1/4″D x 39″H
Woods: Cherry; mahogany
Number of parts: 9
Assembly time: 5–6 hours
Price: $306.00 both woods
Note: Upholstery fabric
  not included.

Kit: Armchair
Period: 1740, Chippendale
Company: The Bartley
  Collection, Ltd.
Dimensions: 24″W
  x 22 3/4″D x 39″H
Woods: Cherry; mahogany
Number of parts: 11
Assembly time: 6 hours
Price: $319.00 both woods
Note: Upholstery fabric
  not included.

Note the Cupid's bow shape of the top rail with rolled ears at the ends, the Gothic arch design of the pierced splat, and the straight legs, all characteristic of Chippendale design.

Kit: Corner chair
Period: Circa 1765, Chippendale
Company: The Bartley Collection, Ltd.
Dimensions: 30 1/2"W x 30 1/2"D x 31"H
Woods: Cherry; mahogany
Number of parts: 23
Assembly time: 4 hours
Price: $299.00 both woods
Note: Upholstery fabric not included.

Corner chairs, also called roundabout chairs, reached their peak under Chippendale.

Kit: Plant stand
Period: Queen Anne
Company: Heath Craft Woodworks
Dimensions: 12" top diameter x 29"H
Wood: Mahogany
Number of parts: 6
Assembly time: 2 hours
Price: $69.95
Note: Hand drill is required; drill bit included with kit.

Kit: Oval candle stand
Period: 1800, Queen Anne
Company: The Bartley Collection, Ltd.
Dimensions: 23"W x 16"D x 27 1/2"H
Woods: Cherry; mahogany
Number of parts: 5
Assembly time: 1 1/2–2 hours
Price: $114.00 both woods

Kit: Candle table
Period: Circa 1750, Queen Anne
Company: The Bartley Collection, Ltd.
Dimensions: 14 1/2" top diameter x 23 1/2"H
Woods: Cherry; mahogany
Number of parts: 6
Assembly time: 1 1/2–2 hours
Price: $90.00 both woods

QUEEN ANNE & CHIPPENDALE KITS (1720–1795)

Kit: Candle stand
Period: Circa 1725, Queen Anne
Company: The Bartley Collection, Ltd.
Dimensions: 10″ top diameter x 40″H
Woods: Cherry; mahogany
Number of parts: 6
Assembly time: 1 1/2–2 hours
Price: $99.00 both woods

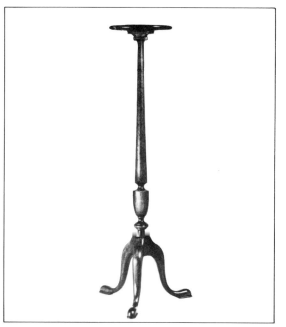

Kit: Old English muffin stand
Period: Circa 1790 (adaptation)
Company: The Bartley Collection, Ltd.
Dimensions: Shelf diameters 10″, 11″, 12″ x 35″H
Woods: Cherry; mahogany
Number of parts: 8
Assembly time: 1 1/2–2 hours
Price: $135.00 both woods

Afternoon tea will never be the same after presenting your cucumber sandwiches and treacle tarts on this impressive display stand. When not in use for tea, it's a perfect showplace for African violets.

Kit: Corner table
Period: Circa 1740 (Virginia), Queen Anne
Company: The Bartley Collection, Ltd.
Dimensions: 27″W x 27″D x 28″H
Woods: Cherry, mahogany
Number of parts: 12
Assembly time: 2–3 hours
Price: $255.00 both woods

Kit: Oval drop-leaf coffee table
Period: Queen Anne (adaptation)
Company: Yield House
Dimensions: 46″W x 31″D (leaves up) x 16 1/2″H; 17″D (leaves down)
Wood: Pine
Number of parts: 17
Assembly time: 3 hours
Price: $129.00

Kit: Drop-leaf table
Period: Circa 1740
Company: The Bartley
　Collection, Ltd.
Dimensions: 43″W x 46″D
　(leaves up) x 29″H
Woods: Cherry; mahogany
Number of parts: 23
Assembly time: 3–5 hours
Price: $445.00 both woods

Kit: Tea table
Period: Circa 1735, Queen
　Anne
Company: The Bartley
　Collection, Ltd.
Dimensions: 31″W
　x 20″D x 27″H
Woods: Cherry; mahogany
Number of parts: 30
Assembly time: 4 hours
Price: $395.00 both woods
　with candle slides;
　$345.00 both woods
　without candle slides

This lovely tea table has been faithfully copied from an original in the Henry Ford Museum in Dearborn, Michigan. Note the raised edge on the top to prevent cups and saucers from slipping off.

Kit: Writing desk
Period: Mid–1700s
　(adaptation)
Company: Emperor Clock
　Company
Dimensions: 59 1/4″W
　x 29″D x 30″H
Wood: Cherry
Number of parts: 68
Assembly time: 8–10
　hours
Price: $449.50

QUEEN ANNE & CHIPPENDALE KITS (1720–1795)

Kit: Butler's tray table
Period: 1720
Company: The Bartley
Collection, Ltd.
Dimensions: 34″W x 22″D
(sides up) x 18 1/2″H
Woods: Cherry; mahogany
Number of parts: 27
Assembly time: 2 hours
Price: $279.00 both woods

Kit: Butler's tray table
Period: Circa 1720, English
Company: The Hardwood
Craftsman, Ltd.
Dimensions: 40″W x 30″D
x 16 1/2″H
Wood: Cherry
Number of parts: 27
Assembly time: 2 hours
Price: $175.00

This butler's tray table lacks the elaborate 11-piece top of Bartley's more expensive kit.

Kit: Commode
Period: Circa 1750,
Chippendale
Company: The Bartley
Collection, Ltd.
Dimensions: 21″W x 18″D
x 29″H
Woods: Cherry; mahogany
Number of parts: 18
Assembly time: 3 hours
Price: $359.00 both woods

This cleverly designed commode, with its handy tray top, is perfect for use as a bedside table or as an occasional piece in the living room.

Kit: End table
Period: Queen Anne
(adaptation)
Company: The Hardwood
Craftsman, Ltd.
Dimensions: 23″W x 18″D
x 22″H
Wood: Cherry
Number of parts: 25
Assembly time: 2–3 hours
Price: $245.00

Kit: End table
Period: Queen Anne
Company: Emperor Clock Co.
Dimensions: 22"W x 26"D x 22"H
Wood: Cherry
Number of parts: 20
Assembly time: 2–3 hours
Price: $149.50

Kit: End table
Period: Queen Anne
Company: Yield House
Dimensions: 17"W x 25"D x 22"H
Wood: Pine
Number of parts: 24
Assembly time: 2–3 hours
Price: $109.00

Kit: Commode
Period: Queen Anne
Company: Emperor Clock Company
Dimensions: 22"W x 26"D x 22"H
Wood: Cherry
Number of parts: 25
Assembly time: 2 1/2 hours
Price: $159.50

Kit: Tray table
Period: Circa 1720, Queen Anne
Company: The Bartley Collection, Ltd.
Dimensions: 28"W x 17 1/2"D x 28"H
Wood: Mahogany
Number of parts: 14
Assembly time: 2 hours
Price: $145.00

QUEEN ANNE & CHIPPENDALE KITS (1720–1795)

Kit: Dining table
Period: Queen Anne
Company: The Bartley Collection, Ltd.
Dimensions: 66″W x 48″D x 29″H
Woods: Cherry, mahogany
Number of parts: 15
Assembly time: 5–6 hours
Price: $810.00 both woods
Note: Two leaves and center section available at additional cost.

Kit: Sideboard
Period: Circa 1750
Company: The Bartley
Collection, Ltd.
Dimensions: 71″W
x 19 1/2″D x 34″H
Woods: Cherry; mahogany
Number of parts: 46
Assembly time: 15–20
hours
Price: $828.00 both woods

QUEEN ANNE & CHIPPENDALE KITS (1720–1795)

Kit: Cupboard
Period: Queen Anne, an adaptation
Company: The Bartley Collection, Ltd.
Dimensions: 71"W x 10 1/2"D x 48"H
Woods: Cherry; mahogany
Number of parts: 13
Assembly time: 8 hours
Price: $450.00 both woods

The sideboard, something of an elongated lowboy, is sold separately in kit form (see previous entry). Later, you can buy the cupboard and mount it on top for a spectacular dining-room piece.

Kit: Hanging cupboard
Period: Eighteenth century
Company: The Bartley Collection, Ltd.
Dimensions: 30"W x 7 3/4"D x 30"H
Wood: Mahogany
Number of parts: 23
Assembly time: 3–4 hours
Price: $185.00

Kit: Lowboy
Period: Mid–1700s
  (adaptation)
Company: Emperor Clock
  Company
Dimensions: 32 1/2″W
  x 18″D x 30 1/4″H
Wood: Cherry
Number of parts: 54
Assembly time: 8 hours
Price: $269.50

Although this piece lacks the details of Bartley's lowboy—namely, the lower finials, keyhole escutcheon, and hand-carved shell motif—it's a true bargain nonetheless, especially considering the solid 3/4″ cherry cabinetry.

Kit: Lowboy
Period: 1750, Queen Anne
Company: The Bartley
  Collection, Ltd.
Dimensions: 34″W x 21″D
  x 31″H
Woods: Cherry; mahogany
Number of parts: 55
Assembly time: 10 hours
Price: $745.00 both woods

The quintessence of Queen Anne kits—and Bartley's exclusive—this is my all-time favorite period piece. Perfect in conception and rendering, it is faithful in every detail, notably the carved fan shape and two turned pendants pointing downward.

Kit: Blockfront chest
Period: Circa 1780,
  Chippendale
Company: The Bartley
  Collection, Ltd.
Dimensions: 36″W x 21″D
  x 31″H
Wood: Mahogany
Number of parts: 69
Assembly time: 5–7 hours
Price: $865.00

Characterized by three vertical blocks (two convex, one concave), these chests were the crowning achievement of the Chippendale period and the hallmark of John Goddard, the most celebrated American cabinetmaker of his day.

Kit: Lady's desk and
  bench
Period: Mid–1700s
Company: The Hardwood
  Craftsman, Ltd.
Dimensions: 38″W x 18″D
  x 30″H (desk); 23″W
  x 18″D x 19″H (bench)
Wood: Cherry
Number of parts: 42
  (desk); 9 (bench)
Assembly time: 2 hours
  (desk); 30 minutes
  (bench)
Price: $439.00 (desk);
  $119.00 (bench)

QUEEN ANNE & CHIPPENDALE KITS (1720–1795)

Kit (left): Secretary
Period: Queen Anne
Company: Emperor Clock Company
Dimensions: 31″W x 20″D x 76 1/2″H
Wood: Cherry; black walnut
Number of parts: 120
Assembly time: 25–30 hours
Price: $499.00 cherry; $649.00 black walnut

The desk is available separately in kit form for $379.00 in cherry and $519.50 in black walnut. The drawers are dovetailed and the drop front and top drawer both lock. Glass is not included.

Kit (far left): Highboy
Period: 1750, Queen Anne
Company: The Bartley Collection, Ltd.
Dimensions: 40 1/2″W x 22 1/4″D x 74″H
Woods: Cherry; mahogany
Number of parts: 270
Assembly time: 45–50 hours
Price: $1390.00 both woods

The flattop style of this highboy is a design carryover from the earlier William and Mary period. At 74 inches tall, this piece will fit splendidly into almost any room.

Kit: Pencil-post bed
Period: Eighteenth
  century
Company: The Bartley
  Collection, Ltd.
Dimensions: 60″W x 82″L
  x 83″H (double)
Woods: Cherry; mahogany
Number of parts: 16
Assembly time: 3–4 hours
Price: $469.00 both woods
Note: Bed is also available
  in single ($439.00) and
  queen size ($495.00).
  Draperies not included.

*On frigid New England
nights, the draperies of this
eighteenth-century bed
were always drawn to pre-
serve warmth; they were
tied back during the day.
The bed takes its name
from the shape of its
slender posts.*

Kit: Old Charleston bench
Period: Victorian
Company: Moultrie
 Manufacturing Co.
Dimensions: 48″W x 15″D
 x 36″H and 96″W x 15″D.
 x 36″H (pictured)
Materials: Cypress and
 cast aluminum
Number of parts: 15 (48″);
 17 (96″)
Assembly time: 2 hours
Price: $225.00 (48″);
 $325.00 (96″)

This bench weathers beautifully in all climates, without any additional finish, and is easily assembled.

TURN OF THE CENTURY KITS (1880–1920)

In the mid-1880s, large furniture factories were built to meet the demands of a growing middle class that needed durable but inexpensive furniture; Grand Rapids, Michigan, was the industry center. Thanks to steam-powered equipment (lathes, for example), complicated turned chairs and fancy pedestal legs could be manufactured in great quantity—at a price within the reach of most buyers. This furniture, fashioned of oak, still turns up in antique shops and attics across the country; as the price of seventeenth-, eighteenth-, and early nineteenth-century antiques rises beyond the means of many collectors, Golden Oak (as it is known) has enjoyed a renewed popularity. Many of the rolltop desks, pedestal tables, and pressback chairs of the period were relegated to the basement or the kitchen once their owners could afford something more elegant, but today they are sought for their rich oak grain and sturdy lines.

Carved claw-and-ball feet are the highlight of the octagonal dining table sold in kit form by Heath Craft Woodworks, the only major company in the kit field concentrating on unassembled pieces inspired by turn-of-the-century designs. Heath Craft, owned by Zenith (and an affiliate of Heathkit Electronics), also offers a spectacularly detailed oak rolltop desk. One distinctive feature is mullions on the back panel—slender bars of wood that give a decorative paneled effect. With its unusual and attractive back, the desk can either serve as a handsome room divider or be pushed against the wall in traditional fashion. The barrister bookshelves offered by Yield House work particularly well with this impressive desk. They probably would have been constructed of mahogany or oak originally, but Yield House sells them in pine—at an extraordinarily reasonable price for shelves with glass doors.

Probably the most unusual piece in this section is the swing rocker kit, built by Paul Saupe in Monticello, Iowa, and based on a chair of his mother's. The rocker, ornately turned and boasting a unique rocking mechanism, is available in walnut, cherry, or maple, with either a caned or upholstered seat and back. Saupe's company, Heritage Design, also manufactures two solid oak serving tables inspired by the furniture designs of the Roycroft Shops, a turn-of-the-century artists' colony in East Aurora, New York. Devoted to hand craftsmanship, the Roycroft Shops excelled in printing, metalworking, and furniture building.

Kit: Country chair
Period: Circa 1900
Company: Peerless Rattan
**Dimensions: 17 1/2"W
x 16 1/2"D x 36"H**
**Wood: American
hardwood**
Number of parts: 12
**Assembly time: 4–6 hours
including seat weaving**
**Price: $30.00 with sea-
grass seat kit**

*Spare, simple lines highlight
this hardwood chair, which
looks right at home in a
country kitchen. You can
choose from sea grass
($6.00, shown), fiber rush
($6.00), flat reed ($6.50),
shaved slab ($6.50), or cane
($9.00) seating materials.
(Shaved slab is 8–9mm
wide binding cane.)*

Kit: Library ladder/chair
**Period: Nineteenth
century**
Company: Yield House
**Dimensions: 16 3/4"W
x 23"D x 36"H**
Wood: Maple
**Number of parts:
Preassembled, shipped
knocked down**
Assembly time: 1/2 hour
Price: $89.00

Kit: Occasional chair
Period: 1880
Company: Peerless Rattan
**Dimensions: 17"W x 17"D
x 31 1/2"H**
**Wood: American
hardwood**
Number of parts: 10
**Assembly time: 8 hours
including seat caning**
Price: $44.95

*Popular as kitchen chairs
during the Victorian period,
this chair and the country
chair opposite were inspired
by eighteenth-century ladderback designs.*

Kit: Pressback armchair
Period: Victorian
**Company: Heath Craft
Woodworks**
**Dimensions: 22"W x 19"D
x 41"H**
Wood: Oak
Number of parts: 26
Assembly time: 3–4 hours
Price: $149.95
**Note: Hand drill required;
drill bit included with
kit. Also available as a
sidechair for $129.95.**

*Smooth, curving arms, a
comfortable carved saddle
seat, and a deeply em-
bossed pattern on the back
are distinctive features of
this Victorian armchair.*

TURN OF THE CENTURY KITS (1880–1920)

Kit: Caned swing rocker
Period: Circa 1876
Company: Heritage Design
Dimensions: 21″W x 28″D x 42″H
Woods: Maple; cherry; walnut (pre-sanded)
Number of parts: 74
Assembly time: 6–8 hours
Price: $276.00 all woods
Note: Tools and materials for hand caning are included. Also available with upholstered back and seat for $228.25. Upholstery materials not included (less than 1 yard of 54-inch wide material required).

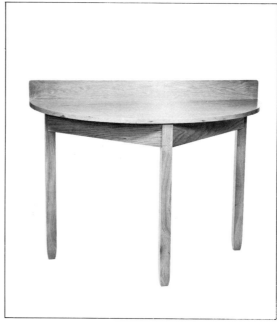

Kit: Roycroft half-round serving table
Period: 1895–1915
Company: Heritage Design
Dimensions: 48″W x 24″D x 36″H
Wood: Oak (other woods on request)
Number of parts: 8
Assembly time: 1 1/2 hours
Price: $138.00

Founded in 1895 in East Aurora, New York, the Roycroft Shops designed and made furniture in the simple, functional style known as Arts and Crafts. Today, original Roycroft pieces fetch high prices at auction.

Kit: Roycroft serving table
Period: 1895–1915
Company: Heritage Design
Dimensions: 44″W x 22″D x 37 1/2″H
Wood: Oak (other woods on request)
Number of parts: 16
Assembly time: 2 hours
Price: $158.00

Kit: Dining table
Period: Victorian
Company: Heath Craft Woodworks
Dimensions: 48″ octagonal top diameter x 29 1/2″H; 64″W (with leaf added)
Wood: Solid oak and oak veneer
Number of parts: 18
Assembly time: 8–10 hours
Price: $495.00
Note: Hand drill is required; drill bit is included with kit.

Note the tenacious grip of the claws on the exposed ball (Chippendale's claw-and-ball motif) at the base of this massive 8-inch-thick pedestal.

Kit: Rolltop desk
Period: Victorian (adaptation)
Company: Heath Craft Woodworks
Dimensions: 58″W x 28″D x 49″H
Wood: White oak and white oak veneer
Number of parts: approximately 200
Assembly time: 40 hours
Price: $995.00
Note: Hand drill required; drill bit included with kit.

This oak rolltop features details that you'd pay up to $2500 for in an antique shop, including egg-and-dart molding, mullioned side and back panels, brass pulls, and 21 pigeonholes.

Kit: Barrister's bookshelves (3 units shown)
Period: Nineteenth century
Company: Yield House
Dimensions: 33 1/2″W x 12 1/2″D x 16 1/4″H (each unit)
Wood: Pine
Number of parts: 9 (each unit)
Assembly time: 1 hour (all units)
Price: $64.00 (1 unit); $119.00 (2 units); $174.00 (3 units)

Kit: Icebox bar
Period: Circa 1900
Company: Yield House
Dimensions: 24″W x 16″D x 38″H
Wood: Pine (plywood side panels)
Number of parts: 63
Assembly time: 3 1/2 hours (KD, simple assembly)
Price: $149.00

Kit: Dr. Evans hall mirror chair
Period: Circa 1900
Company: Yield House
Dimensions: 24″W x 17″D x 72″H
Wood: Pine
Number of parts: 45
Assembly time: 2 hours (KD, simple assembly)
Price: $139.00

TURN OF THE CENTURY KITS (1880–1920)

Kit: Hall mirror
Period: Victorian (mission influence)
Company: Heath Craft Woodworks
Dimensions: 36"W x 3 1/2"D x 17"H
Wood: White oak
Number of parts: 19
Assembly time: 1 1/2 hours
Price: $129.95

Kit: Medicine cabinet
Period: Victorian
Company: Yield House
Dimensions: 15"W x 5 1/2"D x 28 1/2"H (single, as pictured); 29 1/4"W x 5 1/2"D x 28 1/2"H (double)
Wood: Pine
Number of parts: 14
Assembly time: 1 1/2–2 hours
Price: $54.00 (single); $89.00 (double)

Kit: Bookrest
Period: Victorian
Company: Heath Craft Woodworks
Dimensions: 18"W x 12"D x 14"H
Wood: White oak
Number of parts: 14
Assembly time: 2 hours
Price: $69.95
Note: Hand drill required; drill bit included with kit.

Kit: Breadbox
Period: Turn of the century
Company: American Forest Products Company
Dimensions: 18"W x 12"D x 10 1/2"H
Wood: Pine
Number of parts: 8
Assembly time: 1 hour
Price: $24.95

Kit: English carriage clock
Period: Early Colonial
Company: Mason &
Sullivan
Dimensions: 10 7/8″W
x 6 1/8″D x 15 1/2″H
Woods: Mahogany; cherry
Number of parts: 15 (clock
case)
Assembly time: 5–7 hours
Price: $83.00 (cherry);
$108.00 (mahogany);
$145.50 (movement and
moving moon dial)

Clocks like this one were brought to America from England. It is equally attractive on the mantel, a lowboy, bookshelves, or a table.

CLOCKS & MUSICAL INSTRUMENTS

For the truly ambitious (and the very patient), a host of companies offer clocks and musical instruments in un-assembled form. The following section includes a sampling of kits from firms I am familiar with and can recommend to readers without hesitation.

The best prospective candidates for assembling these kits are hobbyists who have a flair for detailed work, whether building furniture for dollhouses or as-sembling model railroad cars. People who have put together a number of fur-niture kits will also find these projects within their capabilities, as we did when we assembled a clavichord.

A caveat with regard to musical in-strument kits: keeping the instruments in tune can be more difficult than as-sembling them. Our clavichord is sensi-tive to even the slightest change in temperature and atmospheric condi-tions, especially humidity, and needs frequent tunings.

As for the kit clock information in this section, keep in mind that the prices quoted rarely include the move-ment and dial. Depending on which type you choose, movements can run almost as much as—or even more than—the clock kit itself. We chose a Westminster chime for our clock, which tolls sonorously on the quarter hour.

Kit: Aaron Willard clock
Period: Circa 1800
Company: Cohasset Colonials
Dimensions: 10″W x 5″D x 36″H
Wood: Pine
Number of parts: 22
Assembly time: 4 hours
Price: $198.00

Aaron Willard and his brother Simon were two of the most celebrated and prolific clockmakers of their day.
This clock, also known as a coffin clock, comes with a completely assembled eight-day movement that is key wound and gongs on the hour.

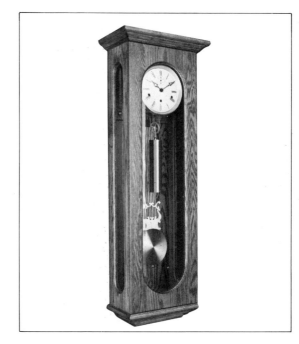

Kit: Vienna regulator
Period: Eighteenth-century European
Company: Westwood Clocks n' Kits
Dimensions: 15″W x 8 1/2″D x 42″H
Woods: Oak; cherry
Number of parts: 6
Assembly time: 6 hours
Price: $299.90 with hour/half-hour strike; $329.90 with Westminster chime every 15 minutes; cherry $20.00 additional.
Note: Beveled glass is available at $89.95 extra.

Kit: Grandfather clock
Period: Mid-1800s
Company: Westwood
  Clocks n' Kits
Dimensions: 22 5/8″W
  x 12 3/4″D
  x 80 3/4″H
Woods: Oak; cherry
Number of parts: 48
Assembly time: 10 hours
Price: $369.95 oak; $419.95
  cherry
Note: Westwood offers
  five movements,
  ranging in price from
  $299.95 to $899.95.
  Beveled glass is
  available at $69.95 extra.

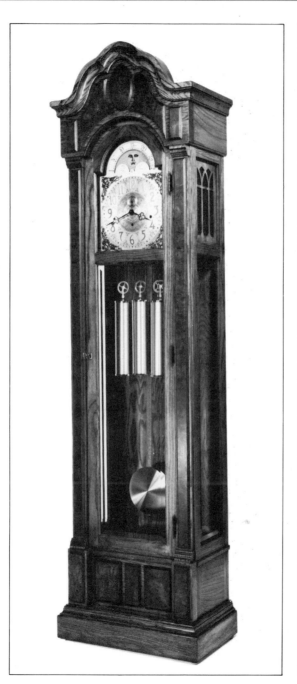

Kit: Cambridge
  grandmother clock
Period: Late 1800s
Company: Craft Products
  Co.
Dimensions: 18 3/8″W
  x 12 1/4″D x 77 1/2″H
Woods: Cherry; walnut
Number of parts: 65 (clock
  case)
Assembly time: 16–20
  hours
Price: $219.50; $269.50
Note: Movements run
  from $110.00 to $219.00;
  dials $47.00–$91.50.

*Note the carved bonnet top
and finial, typical of many
furnishings from the Queen
Anne period. Like the finest
traditional hall clocks, this
one features four graceful
hood pillars on either side
of the face.*

CLOCKS & MUSICAL INSTRUMENTS

Kit: Willard banjo clock
Period: 1802
Company: Mason &
  Sullivan
Dimensions: 10″W
  x 3 3/4″D x 33″H
Woods: Mahogany; walnut
Number of parts: 35 (clock
  case)
Assembly time: 5–6 hours
Price: $192.00 mahogany;
  $205.00 walnut; $48.50
  movement

*Patented in 1802 by Simon
Willard, this lovely clock,
the original of which is at
the Boston Museum of Fine
Arts, is distinguished by its
refined lines.*

Kit: Music stand
Period: Queen Anne
Company: Zuckermann
  Harpsichords, Inc.
Dimensions: Stand 12″W
  x 18″L; height adjustable
  from 34″ to 54″
Wood: Mahogany
Number of parts: 16
Assembly time: 2–3 hours
Price: $78.00 ppd.

Kit: Barometer
Period: Late 1800s
Company: Craft Products
  Co.
Dimensions: 29″H
Woods: Cherry; walnut
Number of parts: 6
Assembly time: 3–4 hours
Price: $64.00; $67.00

Kit: Music box
Period: Traditional
Company: Mason
  & Sullivan
Dimensions: 5 1/2″W
  x 3 3/4″D x 3″H
Wood: Cherry
Number of parts: 11 plus
  movement
Assembly time: 3–4 hours
Price: $29.00 (case); $15.50
  (movement)

Kit: Fretted clavichord
Period: Seventeenth century
Company: Zuckermann Harpsichords, Inc.
Dimensions: 39″W x 11 1/2″D x 27 1/2″H (with stand)
Woods: Mahogany with boxwood/ebony keyboard, spruce soundboard, beech bridge, oak pinblocks
Number of parts: 44 plus keyboard
Assembly time: 25–40 hours
Price: $470.00 (case); $130.00 (stand)

Keyboards on all Zuckermann kits are copied from authentic old instruments and are correctly weighted and balanced. Finishing the natural wood of the cases requires careful sanding, oiling, and polishing.

CLOCKS & MUSICAL INSTRUMENTS

Kit: Italian harpsichord
Period: Eighteenth century
Company: Zuckermann Harpsichords, Inc.
Dimensions: 30"W x 79"D x 32 1/2"H (with stand)
Woods: Yellow cedar with beech stand
Number of parts: 94
Assembly time: 80–120 hours
Price: $1675.00 (includes stand)

Unlike the clavichord, which will remain permanently set once voiced (a procedure that adjusts tone quality and register, not to be confused with tuning), the harpsichord demands revoicing. Builders must also be adept at changing a broken quill (the part that plucks the wire) from time to time.

Kit: Bentside spinet
Period: Eighteenth century, English
Company: Frank Hubbard, Inc.
Dimensions: 30″W x 72″D x 57″H (lid raised)
Wood: Basswood or poplar case parts
Assembly time: Precut kit (all parts ready for gluing) 300 hours; precut kit with assembled case 250 hours; assembled and veneered kit (ready for voicing and musical assembly) 100–150 hours
Price: Precut kit $1650; case assembled $2600; assembled $5880

CLOCKS & MUSICAL INSTRUMENTS

Kit: Fortepiano after Johann Andreas Stein
Period: Circa 1784
Company: Frank Hubbard, Inc.
Dimensions: 38″W x 83 1/2″D x 59″H (lid raised)
Wood: Basswood or poplar case parts
Assembly time: Basic kit 500–600 hours; dimensioned kit (wood cut to thickness and width only) 400–500 hours; precut kit (all parts ready for gluing) 300 hours; precut kit with assembled case 250 hours; assembled and veneered kit (ready for voicing and musical assembly) 100–150 hours
Price: Basic kit $1875; dimensioned kit $2250; precut kit $2850; case assembled $3650; assembled $8200

Kit: Harpsichord after Pascal Taskin
Period: Circa 1769
Company: Frank Hubbard, Inc.
Dimensions: 3'1 3/4"W x 7'7 3/4"D x 66"H (lid raised)
Wood: Basswood or poplar case parts
Assembly time: Basic kit 500–600 hours; dimensioned kit (wood cut to thickness and width only) 400–500 hours; precut kit (all parts ready for gluing) 300 hours; precut kit with assembled case 250 hours; assembled kit (ready for voicing and musical assembly) 100–150 hours
Price: Basic kit $2250; dimensioned kit $2570; precut kit $3000; case assembled $3600; assembled $6100
Note: Harpsichord is also available in a single manual model.

CONTEMPORARY KNOCKDOWN FURNITURE

Kit: Vermont bunkbed
(two twin beds)

Period: Contemporary

Dimensions: 32″W x 82″L
x 41″H (each twin)

Wood: Red oak

Number of parts: 13 (each
bed)

Assembly time: 1 1/2
hours (entire unit)

Price: $710.00 (trundle
$285.00 additional)

Note: Mattresses not
included

Available: At Conran's
stores and by mail

*With the optional trundle,
this space-efficient bed
sleeps three comfortably.*

CONTEMPORARY KNOCKDOWN FURNITURE

As prices for assembled, finished contemporary furniture continue to spiral upward, the market for what the industry calls knockdown, or KD, furniture will no doubt continue to grow. Although KD is a relatively recent development, there are already several types of designs available, among them Bauhaus, butcher block, high-tech, country, even sleek glass-and-brass pieces and a western sling style. The broad range encompasses both casual porch furnishings and formal dining-room pieces.

KD furniture is constructed in such a way that its parts can be broken down after manufacture and packaged unassembled, then put together by the customer after purchase. Assembly is simple. You just tighten a few bolts, overlap joints, or snap parts together. Gluing is hardly ever required, and most KD furniture is sold already stained and finished. So, in the true sense of the word, KD pieces are not kits, which demand gluing and more work to assemble and stain.

Because KD items are usually finished and preassembled in parts, there is, understandably, not as great a savings as with kits. The savings realized with KD runs a more modest 20 percent as opposed to an average savings of 30 to 60 percent with full-fledged kits. KD furniture costs a bit less than showroom furniture because labor and transportation costs are lower.

Just as with reproduction kits, there is a broad price range in KD. For example, unfinished KD pine pieces sold in a lumberyard may require a lot of sanding and will therefore be quite inexpensive. In contrast, a solid brass 3/4-inch glass-top table will seem costly. Details of design, the materials used, and the degree to which the furniture has been finished all play a part in the price.

In addition to cost savings, there are other (and perhaps just as important) motivations for considering KD furniture. Generally when you select a piece from the sales floor, you can take the item (provided it's in stock) with you the same day. It will be packaged in a manageable box, which you can easily maneuver down narrow hallways and past tight corners. If you've ever gotten a table wedged in such a corner, you'll appreciate this quality of KD.

Furniture sold in pieces is especially popular with mobile young people who may move frequently and with businesspeople who want smart but not expensive furnishings for a second-residence apartment near their office. If you're in the mobile category, simply store the empty KD boxes, and when you're ready to move, disassemble your furniture and repack it in the original boxes. Legs are easily removed from tables and chairs; desks and bookcases come apart in half an hour or so; couch joints unsnap and cushions can be stacked in a minimum of space. Chances are good you won't need a huge long-distance moving van or an army of reluctant friends to uproot you.

Although many KD items are available through retailers that specialize in this type of furniture—stores such as Conran's and the Door Store on the East Coast, for example—many department stores across the country now sell KD, including Jordan Marsh in Boston, Foley's stores throughout Texas, and Macy's in New York. I have also found KD lines in Sears, J. C. Penney, home centers, and even lumberyards. To identify KD pieces, check the furniture tags. If the table is KD, the tag will read "To be assembled by the customer," "easy assembly," or simply "KD."

Many knockdown pieces are manufactured abroad, especially in Portugal and Denmark. While researching unassembled modern furniture for this section, two companies kept turning up at several different locations in New York:

Imp and Enrico Bartolini Designs. Both freely use pine and poplar in a natural tone to make such items as trundle beds, loveseats, bookcases, occasional tables of all sorts, and étagères. For marketing reasons, however, the same store rarely, if ever, carries the complete line of a manufacturer. Macy's may feature Imp's pine living-room line, while Conran's may have an exclusive on the bedroom furnishings. To date I've seen few upholstered KD pieces; those I did see had removable cushions.

In general, KD furniture is not as solid and well built as kits you buy and assemble yourself. Butcher block items are an exception; they tend to be quite sturdy. Another exception is the line offered by Design-kit, a newly established firm based in Palisades, New York. Its furniture, all made at the Palisades address, is built of oak, with frames doweled at the shop, to be bolted together by the customer. The pieces are all heavy, solid, and extremely durable. Since Design-kit sells directly to the customer (by mail primarily), the savings as of this writing are considerably more substantial than KD pieces sold retail—the way most lines are marketed. Design-kit leaves its chairs and tables unfinished, which

CONTEMPORARY KNOCKDOWN FURNITURE

also contributes to their lower cost. One of the pieces, a coffee table with a 1 3/8-inch oak top, 36 inches long, costs only $110.00, presanded and unfinished. By comparison, a KD nest of tables, half the size and made of pine, sells at Conran's retail for over $160.00.

If you're in the market for furnishings that will enhance the casual look of a bedroom or living room, or if the high-gloss look of high-tech appeals to you, then I think you'll find knockdown furniture worth investigating. The directory at the back of the book lists retail outlets where you can purchase the pieces pictured in this section. Keep in mind that prices for furniture by the same manufacturer may vary from store to store. And don't be disappointed if a piece you'd like to order turns out not to be available. The lines represented here are fairly stable, but sometimes one line disappears, only to be replaced by another, usually of similar design. The industry is relatively young, and manufacturers are always looking for new ideas.

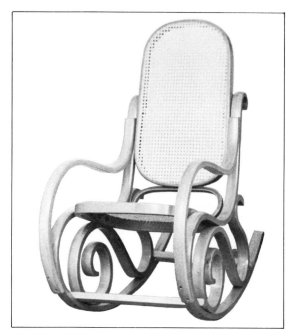

Kit: Bentwood rocker
Period: 1860
Dimensions: 19 1/2"W x 41"D x 42"H
Wood: Beech
Number of parts: 6
Assembly time: 1/2 hour
Price: $135.00
Available: Mail order from Conran's and retail outlets (see buyers' guide)

Although the bentwood rocker dates back to the nineteenth century, when Viennese cabinetmaker Michael Thonet invented a process by which solid pieces of wood could be steam-bent into curves, it has become an extraordinarily popular fixture in contemporary settings.

Kit: Stuns high-back chair
Period: Contemporary
Dimensions: 27"W x 30"D x 33 1/2"H
Materials: Tubular steel frame with cotton-rayon upholstery
Number of parts: 8
Assembly time: 1/2 hour
Price: $165.00
Available: At Conran's stores and by mail

Made in Sweden, this comfortable chair is upholstered in a brown-and-cream "graph" pattern, a blend of cotton, rayon, and flax.

Kit: Couch
Period: Contemporary
Company: Design-kit
**Dimensions: 76″W x 31″D
x 15″H (seat) x 31″H**
**Wood: Oak (unfinished,
machine presanded)**
**Number of parts: 6,
exclusive of slats**
Assembly time: 1 hour
**Price: $308.00 with
cushions; $110.00 frame
only, any length**

**Kit (below): Wedgelock
loveseat**
Period: Contemporary
**Company: Richard
Ehrlich/Wedgelock
Furniture**
**Dimensions: 53″W x 27″D
x 29″H**
**Materials: Solid oak
butcher block sides,
poplar frame, nylon
tweed upholstery**
Number of parts: 5
**Assembly time: 15
minutes**
Price: $400.00
**Note: Also available as a
couch (77″W x 27″D
x 29″H) for $499.00.**

**Kit: British officer's chair
with ottoman (deluxe
model)**
Period: Contemporary
Company: Jensen-Lewis
**Dimensions: 23 1/2″
square x 28 1/2″H
(chair); 23 1/2″ square
(ottoman)**
**Materials: Selected
hardwood and canvas**
**Number of parts: 7 (chair);
5 (ottoman)**
Assembly time: 1/2 hour
**Price: $110.00 (chair);
$75.00 (ottoman)**

The tufted upholstered pillows, which snap onto the seat and back of the chair, are available in rust or sand canvas, Belgian linen, or taupe suedelike Naugahyde.

CONTEMPORARY KNOCKDOWN FURNITURE

Kit: Living room suite
Period: Contemporary
Company: Enrico Bartolini Designs
Dimensions: 75"W x 35"D x 31"H (sofa); 52"W x 35"D x 31"H (loveseat); 51"W x 20"D x 20"H (cocktail table); 23"W x 20"D x 20"H (end table); 30"W x 18"D x 72"H (étagère); 28"W x 35"D x 31"H (chair)
Materials: sugar pine and poplar; cotton duckcloth
Number of parts: 9 (sofa); 7 (loveseat); 5 (cocktail table); 5 (end table); 7 (étagère); 6 (chair)
Assembly time: 1/2 hour average for each piece
Price: $299.00 (sofa); $229.00 (loveseat); $79.00 (cocktail table); $69.00 (end table); $149.00 (étagère); $179.00 (chair)

Kit: Tech living room suite
Period: Contemporary
Dimensions: 57″W x 32″D
x 30″H (loveseat); 33″W
x 32″D x 30″H (armchair);
26″W x 14 1/2″D x 22″H
(trolley); 63″W x 13″D
x 72″H (mesh shelving
unit, as shown)
Materials: Steel tube
frames with cotton
upholstery (loveseat and
armchair); black steel
tubing and perforated
steel shelves (trolley);
black or white steel
mesh framed in wood
and white melamine-
covered chipboard
shelves (shelving)
Number of parts: 12 plus
wood slats for seat
(loveseat); 10 plus wood
slats for seat (armchair);
8 (trolley); 17 (shelving)
Assembly time: 1/2 hour
(loveseat, armchair); 15
minutes (trolley); 45
minutes (shelving)
Price: $495.00 (loveseat);
$295.00 (armchair);
$70.00 (trolley); $279.00
(shelving)
Available: At Conran's
stores and by mail

Covered in gray, stain-resis-
tant cotton, this high-tech
grouping features steel tube
frames lacquered in black
and removable cushion cov-
ers. Also available in camel.

CONTEMPORARY KNOCKDOWN FURNITURE

Kit: Stool/table
Period: Contemporary
Company: Design-kit
Dimensions: 16″ square;
   12″, 18″, 24″, or 30″H
Wood: Oak (unfinished,
   machine presanded)
Number of parts: 4
   exclusive of slats
Assembly time: 1/2 hour
Price: $25.00; $31.00;
   $38.00; $44.00

Kit: Coffee table
Period: Contemporary
Company: Design-kit
Dimensions: 36″ square
   x 16″H
Wood: Oak (unfinished,
   machine presanded)
Number of parts: 5
Assembly time: 1 hour
Price: $110.00

Kit: Buffet table
Period: Contemporary
Company: Design-kit
Dimensions: 60″W x 18″D
   x 28 1/2″H
Wood: Oak (unfinished,
   machine presanded)
Number of parts: 6
Assembly time: 1 hour
Price: $146.00

Kit: Hi-low table
Period: Contemporary
Company: Woodcutter by Cutter Furniture Corp.
Dimensions: 34″ square x 29″H (high), 17″ (low height)
Wood: Red oak with natural or stained finish
Number of parts: 2
Assembly time: 10 minutes
Price: $99.00

Kit: Gallery square table
Period: Contemporary
Dimensions: 38″ square x 15″H
Materials: Glass top; chrome-plated legs
Number of parts: 5
Assembly time: 15 minutes
Price: $195.00
Available: At Conran's stores and by mail

Kit: Lattice-top table
Period: Contemporary
Dimensions: 36″ square x 16″H
Materials: Birch, with bentwood legs
Number of parts: 5
Assembly time: 1/2 hour
Price: $225.00
Available: At Conran's stores and by mail

The attractive lattice pattern in the solid birch top of this table is accented by the graceful curve of the bentwood legs.

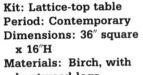

Kit: Rectangular cocktail table
Period: Contemporary
Company: Heath Craft Woodworks
Dimensions: 48″W x 24″D x 16″H
Materials: 3/4″ plate glass; solid brass; heavy brass-plated castings
Number of brass parts: 33
Assembly time: 2 hours
Price: $395.00

CONTEMPORARY KNOCKDOWN FURNITURE

Kit: Four-drawer desk
Period: Contemporary
Company: American
    Forest Products
    Company
Dimensions: 33 5/16″W
    x 13 13/16″D x 28 3/16″H
Wood: Pine
Number of parts: 50
Assembly time: 3 hours
Price: $54.95

Kit: Desk
Period: Contemporary
Company: Woodcutter by
    Cutter Furniture Corp.
Dimensions: 40″W x 20″D
    x 29 1/2″H
Wood: Red oak with white
    laminated top, natural or
    stained finish
Number of parts: 4
Assembly time: 1/2 hour
Price: $165.00

*There's plenty of storage in
this unique desk, with its
solid oak frame and lami-
nated top. Makes a useful
work table and assembles
quickly with six fasteners.*

Kit: Student desk with
    Norway side chair
Period: Contemporary
Company: Imp
Dimensions: 21 1/2″W
    x 21 1/2″D x 28″H
Wood: Pinheiro
    (Portuguese pine) with
    white melamine top
Number of parts: 4 (desk);
    6 (chair)
Assembly time: 1 hour
Price: $250.00 including
    chair; chair sold
    separately for $85.00

*Pinheiro pine trees grow
along the coast of Portugal.
Their wood is harder than
pine found in the United
States because one side of
the tree is exposed to rough
ocean winds and moisture.*

Kit: A-frame drawing table with Norway side chair
Period: Contemporary
Company: Imp
Dimensions: 60″W x 29″D x 28″H (table); 16″W x 13″D x 30″H (chair)
Wood: Pinheiro (Portuguese pine) legs, white melamine top (table); pinheiro (chair)
Number of parts: 11 (table); 6 (chair)
Assembly time: 1 hour (table); 6 (chair)
Price: $415.00 (table); $85.00 (chair)

Kit: Artist drafting table
Period: Contemporary
Company: Enrico Bartolini Designs
Dimensions: 36″W x 31″D x 30″H
Woods: Pine and poplar ("mica" top)
Number of parts: 5
Assembly time: 1/2 hour
Price: $99.00

This is an exceptionally good buy in a drafting ta-ble. Similar models are sold assembled in art stores for up to three times the price.

Kit: Drawing table with high-back chair
Period: Contemporary
Company: Imp
Dimensions: 63″W x 39 1/2″D x 34 3/4″H (table); 18 1/2″ square x 39 1/2″H (chair)
Wood: Solid pinheiro (Portuguese pine)
Number of parts: 18 (table); 8 (chair)
Assembly time: 1 1/2 hours
Price: $660.00 both pieces

CONTEMPORARY KNOCKDOWN FURNITURE

Kit: A-frame junior desk
Period: Contemporary
Company: Imp
Dimensions: 43"W x 24"D x 71"H
Wood: Solid pinheiro (Portuguese pine) with white melamine shelves
Number of parts: 6
Assembly time: 1/2 hour
Price: $340.00

Kit: A-frame bookcase
Period: Contemporary
Company: Imp
Dimensions: 43"W x 16"D x 71"H
Wood: Solid pinheiro (Portuguese pine), white melamine shelves
Number of parts: 9
Assembly time: 1/2 hour
Price: $320.00

Kit: Folding shelf unit (2 units side by side shown)
Period: Contemporary
Dimensions: 26"W x 11"D x 38"H (each unit)
Materials: Beech (presanded, unfinished)
Number of parts: Packed flat, unfolds
Assembly time: 10 minutes
Price: $49.00 per unit
Available: At Conran's stores and by mail

These units can be stacked on top of one another or, as shown here, arranged side by side. A terrific value for solid beech.

Kit: Low stereo cabinet
Period: Contemporary
Dimensions: 48"W x 16"D x 20"H
Materials: White melamine on chipboard
Number of parts: 9
Assembly time: 1/2 hour
Price: $139.00
Available: At Conran's stores and by mail

Kit: Canvas-metal-wood coordinates
Period: Contemporary
Company: Jensen-Lewis
Dimensions: 48″W x 20″D x 28 1/2″H (desk); 24″W x 17 1/2″D x 24″H (3-drawer stacking unit); 24″W x 17 1/2″D x 24″H (drawer-shelf stacking unit)
Materials: Canvas; wood; chrome
Number of parts: 5 (desk); 3 (chair); 5 (3-drawer unit); 3 (drawer-shelf stacking unit)
Assembly time: 1/2 hour each unit
Price: $215.00 (desk); $95.00 (chair); $150.00 (3-drawer unit); $95.00 (drawer-shelf unit)

CONTEMPORARY KNOCKDOWN FURNITURE

Kit: Unfinished shelving
   P.D.Q. (basic unit,
   extension, 2-door
   cabinet, drawer unit,
   and desk/bar unit)
Period: Contemporary
Dimensions: 71"W x 15"D
   x 72"H (as shown)
Materials: Sanded,
   unfinished pine
Number of parts: 25
Assembly time: 1 1/2
   hours
Price: $341.70
Available: At Conran's
   stores and by mail

Kit: Kubus (6 cube units, 4 drawers, 1 set wood doors, 2 sets glass doors, 2 shelves, record divider plus base)
Period: Contemporary
Dimensions: 54"W x 14 1/4"D x 81"H (as shown); each cube 27"W x 14 1/4"D x 27"H
Materials: Pine veneer or white lacquer
Number of parts: 60
Assembly time: 1 1/2 hours
Price: $925.00
Available: At Conran's stores and by mail

Made in Sweden, this add-on cube unit is available in natural pine veneer or white lacquer. It looks wonderful in the living room, den, or kitchen.

CONTEMPORARY KNOCKDOWN FURNITURE

Kit (left): Open shelf system (2 units pictured)
Period: Contemporary
Company: Jensen-Lewis
Dimensions: 36″W x 15″D x 72″H (each unit)
Wood: Unfinished pine
Number of parts: 6 (each unit)
Assembly time: 1 hour
Price: $85.00 per unit
Note: The 2-drawer unit and 2-door cabinet (pictured) are available at $49.95 (drawer) and $57.95 (cabinet).

For an attractive decorator look, staple fabric onto back of rack and give your plants a colorful backdrop.

Kit (right): Etagères and connector with side chairs
Period: Contemporary
Company: Enrico Bartolini Designs
Dimensions: 106″W x 18″D x 72″H (as pictured); 30″W x 18″D x 72″H (étagère only); 48″W x 33″D x 34″H (chair)
Wood: Pine
Number of parts: 7 (étagère); 3 (connector); 5 (chair); 1 (bar/desk)
Assembly time: 2 hours
Prices: $149.00 (étagère, each); $79.00 (connector); $69.00 (chair); $99.00 (bar/desk unit); $614.00 (entire unit as pictured)

CONTEMPORARY KNOCKDOWN FURNITURE

Kit: Plant rack
Period: Contemporary
Company: Jensen-Lewis
Dimensions: 27"W x 20"D
  x 66"H
Materials: Selected
  hardwood
Number of parts: 8
Assembly time: 45
  minutes
Price: $64.00

Kit: Plant tower
Period: Contemporary
Company: Woodworks Ltd.
Dimensions: 18" square
  x 66"H
Wood: Appalachian red
  oak
Number of parts: 16
Assembly time: 1/2 hour
Price: $24.95 ppd.
Note: Tower can be used
  as two separate stands,
  each 36" tall.

Kit: Speaker stand
Period: Contemporary
Company: Woodworks Ltd.
Dimensions: 18″W x 18″D
   x 18″H
Wood: Appalachian red
   oak
Number of parts: 12
   identical parts
Assembly time: 1/2 hour
Price: $12.50 each or
   $24.95 per pair ppd.

Kit: Modular album rack (2
   modules stacked with
   top)
Period: Contemporary
Company: Woodworks Ltd.
Dimensions: 36″W x 18″D
   x 36″H
Wood: Appalachian red
   oak
Number of parts: 17 parts
   per module plus one
   laminated oak top
Assembly time: 1 hour
Price: $79.95 ppd.
Note: These stacking units
   are also available
   separately, either with
   the 3/4″ laminated oak
   top ($49.95 ppd.) or
   without ($34.95 ppd.).

Kit: Spare chair
Period: Contemporary
Company: Woodcutter by
   Cutter Furniture Corp.
Dimensions: 18″ square
   x 31″H
Wood: Red oak with
   natural or stained finish
Number of parts: 12
Assembly time: 45
   minutes
Price: $39.00

*These chairs are far more
comfortable—and not much
more expensive—than
wood or metal folding
chairs. The fabric seat and
back are available in rust,
navy, sand, or brown.*

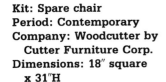

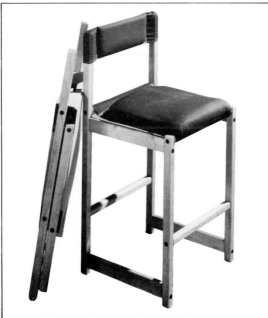

Kit: Spare stool
Period: Contemporary
Company: Woodcutter by
   Cutter Furniture Corp.
Dimensions: 18″ square
   x 36″H
Wood: Red oak with
   natural or stained finish
Number of parts: 7
Assembly time: 1/2 hour
Price: $49.00

CONTEMPORARY KNOCKDOWN FURNITURE

Kit: Life-style chair
Period: Contemporary
Company: J&D Brauner
Dimensions: 17″ square
  x 31″H
Wood: Beech
Number of parts: 6
Assembly time: 1/2 hour
Price: $44.00

The padded seat is covered in saddle-tan vinyl.

Kit: Town and country
  chair
Period: Contemporary
Company: J&D Brauner
Dimensions: 16″ square
  x 32″H
Wood: Beech
Number of parts: 6
Assembly time: 1/2 hour
Price: $49.00

Kit: Elm dining chair
Period: Contemporary
Dimensions: 18″W
  x 17 1/2″D x 38″H
Materials: Elm legs, with
  cotton, rayon velvet
  upholstery
Number of parts: 2
Assembly time: 15
  minutes
Price: $250.00
Available: At Conran's
  stores and by mail

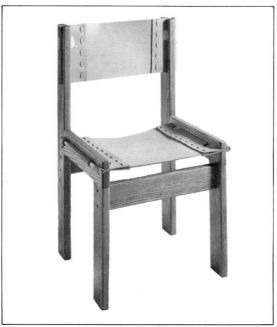

Kit: Sling dining
  chair
Period: Contemporary
Company: Design-kit
Dimensions: 18 3/4″W
  x 19 1/2″D x 34 3/4″H
Materials: Oak and
  leather
Number of parts: 4 wood,
  6 leather
Assembly time: 2 hours
  including seat lacing
Price: $91.00

Kit: Bauhaus chair
Period: Circa 1920
Dimensions: 19″W
  x 22 1/2″D x 31″H
Materials: Beech with
  chrome frame
Number of parts: 5 (side
  chair); 7 (armchair)
Assembly time: 1/2 hour
Price: $60.00 (side
  chair); $75.00 (armchair)
Available: At Conran's
  stores and by mail
Note: Sold KD only by
  mail order; comes
  assembled at stores.

Also known as the Breuer chair after its creator Marcel Breuer, this chair takes its design inspiration from Thonet's bentwood rocker.

CONTEMPORARY KNOCKDOWN FURNITURE

Kit (left): Slat armchair
Period: Contemporary
Company: Design-kit
Dimensions: 27 1/2″W
  x 28″D x 28 3/4″H
Materials: Oak
Number of parts: 4
  (exclusive of slats)
Assembly time: 1 hour
Price: $56.00

Kit (center): Upholstered armchair
Period: Contemporary
Company: Design-kit
Dimensions: 27 1/2″W
  x 28″D x 28 3/4″H
Materials: Oak and 1″
  thick foam covered with
  duck
Number of parts: 5
Assembly time: 1 hour
Price: $66.00

Kit: Dining table with slat dining chairs
Period: Contemporary
Company: Design-kit
Dimensions: 60″W (or
  72″W) x 36″D x 27 1/2″H
  (table); 18 3/4″W
  x 19 3/4″D
  x 34 3/4″H (chair)
Wood: Oak (unfinished,
  machine presanded)
Number of parts: 4 (table);
  4 (chair, exclusive of
  slats)
Assembly time: 1 hour
  (table); 45 minutes
  (chair)
Price: $193.00 (60″ table);
  $214.00 (72″ table);
  $49.50 (chair)

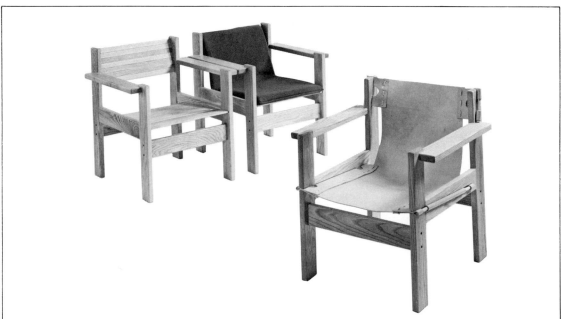

Kit (right): Sling armchair
Period: Contemporary
Company: Design-kit
Dimensions: 27 1/2″W
  x 26″D x 29″H
Materials: Oak and
  leather
Number of parts: 10
Assembly time: 2 hours
  including seat lacing
Price: $140.00

Design-kit even provides the Allen wrench to tighten the socket head bolts.

Kit: Random oak round
   table
Period: Contemporary
Company: J&D Brauner
Dimensions: 30″ diameter
   x 30″H
Wood: Oak
Number of parts: 6
Assembly time: 1/2 hour
Price: $165.00 (as shown)
Note: Table is available in
   four larger sizes.

Kit: Random oak
   rectangular table
Period: Contemporary
Company: J&D Brauner
Dimensions: 48″W x 30″D
   x 30″H
Wood: Oak
Number of parts: 4
Assembly time: 1/2 hour
Price: $190.00 (as shown)
Note: Table is available in
   several different sizes.

*In both styles, the oak has
been hand-rubbed with
natural oils to preserve its
finish.*

Kit: Butcher block table
   and life-style stool
Period: Contemporary
Company: J&D Brauner
Dimensions: 48″W x 24″D
   x 36″H (table); 17″
   square x 24″H (stool)
Materials: Maple and
   hardwood (table); beech
   with saddle-tan vinyl
   seat (chair)
Number of parts: 9 (table);
   10 (chair)
Assembly time: 1/2 hour
   (table); 1/2 hour (chair)
Price: $210.00 (table as
   shown); $59.00 (chair)
Note: Table is available in
   10 different sizes, up to
   72″W x 36″D, at both 36″
   work height and 30″ dining height. Center
   drawer, $35.00.

Kit: Rectangular table
Period: Contemporary
Company: J&D Brauner
Dimensions: 48″W x 30″D
   x 30″H
Wood: Maple
Number of parts: 9
Assembly time: 1/2 hour
Price: $170.00 (as shown)
Note: Table is available in
   three larger sizes.

CONTEMPORARY KNOCKDOWN FURNITURE

Kit: Solid oak rollaway
Period: Contemporary
Company: J&D Brauner
Dimensions: 30″W x 18″D
x 34″H
Wood: Oak
Number of parts: 5
Assembly time: 1/2 hour
Price: $189.00 (as shown)
Note: Also available in 18″
square x 34″H.

Carve meat on the solid oak top, with its grooved surface to catch juices, then wheel your dinner right to the table.

Kit: Work counter
Period: Contemporary
Dimensions: 36″W x 24″D
x 36″H
Materials: Maple
Number of parts: 14
Assembly time: 1 hour
Price: $275.00
Available: At Conran's
stores and by mail

Kit: Pantry table
Period: Contemporary
Company: J&D Brauner
Dimensions: 24″W x 18″D
x 36″H
Materials: Maple and
plated steel
Number of parts: 7
Assembly time: 45
minutes
Price (as shown): $150.00
(without drop leaves or
casters); $265.00 (with
drop leaves and casters)
Note: Table is available in
six different sizes, up to
24″W x 48″L.

Kit: Chopping block
Period: Contemporary
Company: J&D Brauner
Dimensions: 18″ square
x 12″ thick x 34″H
Wood: Maple
Number of parts: 5
Assembly time: 1/2 hour
Price: $175.00

Kit: Country kitchen
Period: Contemporary
Dimensions: Base units
   42″W x 21″D x 27 1/2″H;
   wall cupboard 42″W
   x 12″D x 19″H
Materials: Solid pine with
   polyurethaned veneered
   side panels
Number of parts: Base
   unit, 10; wall cupboard,
   7
Assembly time: 1/2 hour,
   base; fifteen minutes,
   cupboard
Price: $2471 (as shown)
Available: At Conran's
   stores and by mail

CONTEMPORARY KNOCKDOWN FURNITURE

Kit: Storage bench
Period: Contemporary
Company: American
    Forest Products
    Company
Dimensions: 35″W
    x 16 1/4″D x 22 3/8″H
Wood: Pine
Number of parts: 34
Assembly time: 1 1/2
    hours
Price: $44.95

Kit: Three-drawer chest
Period: Contemporary
Company: American
    Forest Products
    Company
Dimensions: 24 5/8″W
    x 13 13/16″D x 28 3/16″H
Wood: Pine
Number of parts: 44
Assembly time: 2 hours
Price: $49.95

Kit: Five-drawer chest
Period: Contemporary
Company: American
    Forest Products
    Company
Dimensions: 24 5/8″W
    x 13 13/16″D
    x 40 15/16″H
Wood: Pine
Number of parts: 64
Assembly time: 2 1/2
    hours
Price: $69.95

Kit: End table
Period: Contemporary
Company: Yield House
Dimensions: 23 1/2″W
    x 19 1/2″D x 23″H
Wood: Pine
Number of parts: 24
Assembly time: 2 hours
Price: $99.00

Also available in a coffee-table style for $119.00, this end table features button pegging on the shelves and brass-finish drawer pulls.

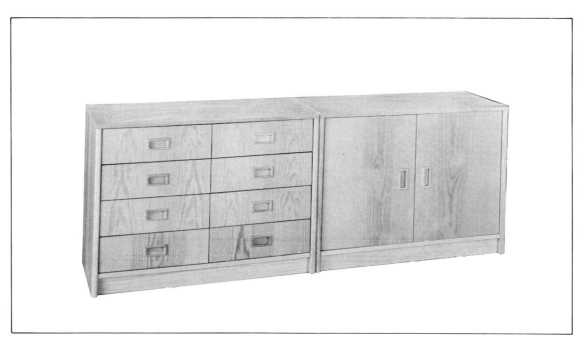

Kit: Eight-drawer chest
  with two-door cabinet
Period: Contemporary
Company: Imp
Dimensions: 38″W
  x 17 1/2″D x 27″H
  (chest); 38″W x 17 1/2″D
  x 27″H (cabinet)
Wood: Pinheiro (Portuguese pine)
Number of parts: 46
  (chest); 8 (cabinet)
Assembly time: 1 hour
  (chest); 1/2 hour
  (cabinet)
Price: $250.00 (chest);
  $155.00 (cabinet)

Kit: Four-drawer chest
  with upper base unit
Period: Contemporary
Company: Imp
Dimensions: 37″W
  x 15 1/2″D x 26″H
  (chest); 37″W x 15 1/2″D
  x 26″H (upper base)
Wood: Pinheiro
  (Portuguese pine)
Number of parts: 34
  (chest); 5 (upper base)
Assembly time: 1 hour
  (chest); 1/2 hour (upper
  base)
Price: $250.00 (chest);
  $155.00 (upper base)

CONTEMPORARY KNOCKDOWN FURNITURE

Kit: Single bed
Period: Contemporary
Company: Imp
Dimensions: 40″W x 76″L
Wood: Pinheiro pine
Number of parts: 8
Assembly time: 1 hour
**Price: $175.00 (mattress
   not included)**

Kit: Double bunkbed
Period: Contemporary
Company: Imp
**Dimensions: 41″W x 77″L
   x 51″H**
**Wood: Pinheiro (Portu-
   guese pine)**
Number of parts: 19
**Assembly time: 1 1/2
   hours**
**Price: $470.00 (mattresses
   not included)**

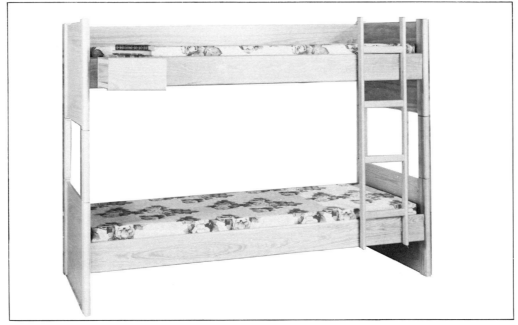

Kit: Bow house
Period: Late 1700s,
   Colonial
Company: Bow House, Inc.
Dimensions: As shown,
   footage 1340 square feet
Wood: Cedar frame
Includes: Approximately
   6000 parts including
   cedar siding, white
   cedar roofing, roof
   rafters, floors, stairs,
   exterior/interior doors,
   stain
Assembly time:
   Depending on number
   of workers and their
   experience, anywhere
   from 3 to 8 weeks
Price: $19,775 (note: total
   cost of half cape house is
   estimated at $60,000–
   65,000, which includes
   allowances for
   foundation, septic tank,
   plumbing and wiring,
   appliances, kitchen
   cabinets, insulation, and
   plasterboard)

KIT HOUSES

There's no question about it: you get more for less when you buy a house in kit form—and a new movement is definitely afoot in the building industry in response to the outrageously high cost of houses today.

If you want a house that doesn't look like one of those ubiquitous models with an "Open for Inspection" sign on the outside, but you're not up to tackling your own construction from scratch, a precut house kit could be the happy middle-ground solution for you. Because kit manufacturers often tailor house plans to suit individual buyers, there are rarely two identical kit houses. So you need not be concerned about buying a package that will look exactly like your neighbor's.

Kit companies ship components of houses to your building site, which must be prepared for raising the house. Some kits arrive on flatbed trucks; one company will even ship your house in manageable 100-pound loads in the event you want to transport it yourself to your remote retreat.

The do-it-yourself aspect of kit houses can cut as much as 10 to 30 percent off construction costs (which represent about 65 percent of the cost of a one-family house, the remaining 35 percent being land and financing).

Much of what you will save depends on the extent to which you are willing to become involved in the actual labor. If you contract out most of the work, your savings will naturally be less.

How long does all this take? Again, that depends. With a little help from their friends, one family spent three months raising their three-bedroom Early American-style house. Others have spent as little as three weeks from foundation to key turning, with a lot of outside help.

Even if you save only 10 percent, there's a good chance you'll end up with a more solidly built structure, perhaps one with a few unique details that you could never have afforded if the house had been built by a contractor. For example, some kit manufacturers include special—and costly—materials your local contractor most likely would not use.

Obbligato requirement: read kit house literature very carefully. In most cases the kit price does *not* include such items as land, plumbing, heating, foundation, septic system, interior decoration, and kitchen appliances. Many brochures will list kit package prices for the basic components, along with an estimate of what the completed house will cost, taking land and other major costs into consideration.

A few things to watch out for: make certain your building site is guarded once materials have been delivered, or you may never have the opportunity to put the pieces together. It's happened. Give preference, also, to companies that give advice freely during building. Reliable companies will see you through to the end—unfinished kit houses make both owners and banks unhappy. If the kit house you choose has a heating system included in the price, bear in mind that in many areas of the country, electric heat is the easiest to install but the most expensive to use. If possible, plan on some sort of supplementary wood heat—a wood-burning stove is more efficient than a fireplace. Be sure to work out the type of insulation to use while your house is being built, not after the champagne has been uncorked.

The foundation is a critical part of any house, so make sure yours will keep the house dry and stable. The kind of foundation you choose will depend on the frost line, the water table, and the angle of the land. Beware of knots in wood—they weaken it—and watch out for any indication of rot. Keep in mind that green lumber, unseasoned, will shrink as it dries, caus-

ing possible warpage. Depending on where unseasoned wood is used in construction, it could mean trouble.

Above all, ask a lot of questions of the representatives from companies whose houses appeal to you most. Find out exactly what the kit price does and doesn't include. Check grades of wood. The more complete the package, the more questions you should be prepared to ask.

Don't rush any phase of the kit house process—from reading over the materials to selecting the actual house and building it. Plan to spend many evenings reading through pamphlets and researching different aspects. Talk to people who have built houses from kits (reputable firms will supply you with a list of customers in your area).

Once you've made your decision, the steps that follow will be very similar to a normal house closing. You'll put down a deposit, obtain a bank mortgage or construction loan, sign a final contract, set a delivery date, make another deposit, and pay in full for final delivery, most likely by certified check.

I think you will be as surprised as I was by the different types of housing now available in kit form, everything from simple sheds to energy-efficient solar houses. By the way, most kit solar

KIT HOUSES

houses feature what is called passive—as opposed to active—solar energy systems. Houses designed to take advantage of passive energy are designed, constructed, and situated in such a way (with center chimneys, lots of glass on the south-facing side, and triple-glazed windows on the other sides, among other features) that the house absorbs solar energy during the day and retains it for a number of hours before releasing it as heat at night. (Active solar units, on the other hand, depend on an outside energy source to collect, store, and distribute heat; they are far more costly to install and maintain than passive units.)

For a complete guide to companies that manufacture kit houses, get a copy of *Guide to Manufactured Homes,* published by the National Association of Home Manufacturers, 6521 Arlington Boulevard, Falls Church, VA 22042, for $4.00.

Kit: Plymouth A model
Period: Eighteenth century (adaptation)
Company: Real Log Homes
Dimensions: As shown, footage 1552 square feet
Wood: Pine
Includes: Precut log package only. Plans included for foundation, joist layouts, floor plans, rafter systems, and elevations. Blueprints detail all dimensions and sill details. Package includes: exterior log walls and gable ends; 28″ x 18″ louvers; pre-hung exterior doors and windows; timber girders and ceiling joists; porch rafters, sills, posts and plates; ridgepoles, 4 x 6 collar ties, 4 x 8 and 2 x 8 gambrel rafters, 4 x 8 purlins and lockspline.
Assembly time: Estimated 2–5 weeks with four people working, depending upon familiarity and skill
Price: As shown $16,900; other models from $9,300–$33,200

KIT HOUSES

Kit: Sam Adams
Period: Colonial
Company: Northern Homes, Inc.
Dimensions: 2168 square feet plus garage
Wood: White fir frame, spruce/pine, with plywood sheathing
Includes: All wood members, hardware, doors, windows, insulation, and roofing; walls are prefabricated; floors are pre-cut
Assembly time: 2–3 months to key turning, depending on amount of work subcontracted
Price: $45,053

Kit: Thomas Jefferson
Period: Colonial
Company: Northern
  Homes, Inc.
Dimensions: 2408 square
  feet, plus garage
Wood: White fir frame,
  spruce/pine, with
  plywood sheathing
Includes: All wood
  members, hardware,
  doors, windows,
  insulation, and roofing
Assembly time: 2–3
  months to key turning,
  depending on amount of
  work subcontracted
Price: $38,764
Note: Kit price includes
  sloped ceiling in second-
  floor bedroom.

KIT HOUSES

Kit: Solar Cascade II
Period: Contemporary
Company: Justus Homes
Dimensions: 60′L x 26′W
   (garage 30′D x 40′W)
Wood: Cedar
Includes: All wood
   members, windows and
   doors, trim and casing,
   cedar shakes, stairs,
   balusters and railings,
   glue, nails, and blue-
   prints
Assembly time: 60–75
   days
Price: $47,000 (Note: Full
   solar system
   approximately $20,000.
   Turn-key price averages
   $100,000 [exclusive of
   solar system],
   depending on amount of
   work contracted and
   labor costs in different
   areas of the country.)

Kit: N-38 Solar Home
Period: Contemporary
Company: Green
Mountain Home
Dimensions: 1264 square
feet, plus entrance way
Wood: Plywood exterior;
pine interior post and
beams
Includes: Enough parts to
complete basic exterior
structure, plus windows,
doors, interior post, and
beams
Assembly time: 2 weeks
Price: $45,000 contractor-
finished price; $6000
less if you complete
work yourself
Note: Price does not
include land, septic
system, well, or site
improvements. Entire
home acts as a solar
collector; heating
system can be reversed
for summer cooling.

KIT HOUSES

Kit: Greenhouse
Period: Contemporary
Company: Lord & Burnham
Dimensions: 9'9"W
    x 21'5"L
Materials: Aluminum and
    glass
Includes: All parts
    prefabricated and
    delivered in
    approximately ten
    separate packages,
    ready to be bolted and
    screwed together
Assembly time: 100 hours
Price: $3037 (as shown)
Note: Greenhouses
    available in eight
    standard lengths from 8
    feet to 26 feet.
    Greenhouses can also be
    used as extra rooms or
    as an enclosure for hot
    tubs, porches, etc.
    Models also available
    with insulated glass.

DECORATING WITH KITS

Country kitchen:
6 kits totaling $348.70 without cabinets; 9 kits totaling $845.70 with cabinets.
Country chairs with woven sea grass seats, Peerless Rattan, $30.00 each; small Salem table, Cohasset Colonials, $172.00; Shaker spice cupboard, Yield House, $49.50; rolltop bread box, American Forest Products Co., $24.95; pots and plants holder, Woodcraft Supply Corp., $42.25; kitchen cabinets (partially assembled, unfinished pine, no hardware or knobs), Carroll Industries, available at local lumberyards and hardware stores; oven cabinet $59.00; 2-door base $229.00; 2-door top $209.00 (other standard units also available).

SHAKER DINING ROOM

**Shaker dining room:
10 kits totaling $781.50.
Shawl-back rocker, Shaker
Workshops, $125.00;
round-top candle stand,
Shaker Workshops, $42.50;
half round table, Cohasset
Colonials, $59.00; window
rod and brackets, Cohasset
Colonials, $7.00 per win-
dow set; harvest table,
Cohasset Colonials,
$265.00; Shaker side chairs
with rushed seat kits,
Cohasset Colonials, $69.00
each.**

*Accessories (not available
as kits): Shaker clock, Brian
Considine, Cabinetmaker,
Post Mills, VT 05058; pew-
ter candlesticks and plates,
courtesy of Gage & Tollner
Restaurant, Brooklyn, NY
11201; wooden trencher,
hooked rug, hen, (hanging)
sifter, framed quilt square,
heart sconces, wooden pig,
Pineapple Primitives, 35
Pineapple St., Brooklyn, NY
11201; tab curtains (lined),
Cohasset Colonials, custom
made to size.*

**Colonial bedroom:
7 kits totaling $911.50:
Candle stand, Cohasset
Colonials, $28.00; four-
poster canopy full-size
bed, Cohasset Colonials,
$259.00; straight chair,
Shaker Workshops, $67.50;
chest of drawers, Cohasset
Colonials, $359.00; quilt
(or towel) rack, Yield
House, $34.00; blanket
chest, Cohasset Colonials,
$139.00; 2′ x 3′ crocheted
rag rug, Country Rag
Rugs, $25.00.**

*Accessories (not available
as kits): pewter-finish lamp,
Old Guilford Forge, Guilford,
CT 16437; canopy/shams,
bedspread, Country Curtains,
The Red Lion Inn,
Stockbridge, MA 01262.*

CONTEMPORARY LIVING ROOM

Two views of the same contemporary living room: 6 kits totaling $976.90. Director's chairs, $49.95, Conran's, New York; love-seat, Enrico Bartolini Designs, $229.00, Joskes, San Antonio and elsewhere; trundle bed, Imp, $435.00, Robinson's, Florida; nest of tables, $169.00, Conran's, New York; stool/table, Design-kit, $44.00, by mail.

Accessories: paper window blinds, Conran's.

CONTEMPORARY DINING NOOK

Contemporary dining nook:
4 kits totaling $398.00.
Round butcher block table,
$255.00, Conran's, New
York; slat dining chairs,
Design-kit, by mail,
$49.50; stool/table, Design-
kit, by mail, $44.00.

Accessories: table lamp,
Conran's.

Contemporary bedroom: 3 kits totaling $795.00. Junior desk, Imp, $340.00, Macy's, New York and others; bentwood rocker, $135.00, Conran's, New York; A-frame bookcase, Imp, $320.00, Jordan Marsh, Boston and others.

Accessories: desk lamp, Conran's; platform bed, Gothic Cabinet Craft, 570 Amsterdam Ave., New York, NY 10024.

QUEEN ANNE LIVING ROOM

Queen Anne living room: 3 kits totaling $1369.50. Drop-leaf table, The Bartley Collection, Ltd., $420.00; coffee table, Emperor Clock Company, $169.50; lowboy, The Bartley Collection, Ltd., $780.00.

Accessories (not available as kits): wing chair, Macy's, New York; oil paintings (left and right) by Jeff Geary, Brooklyn, NY and (center) by Derek James, Brooklyn, NY; plant stand, Littlejohn's; sample chest, spoon rack, and candlesticks, Rollingswood.

PUTTING IT ALL TOGETHER

PUTTING IT ALL TOGETHER

BEFORE YOU BEGIN

The key ingredients in kit building—component pieces, instructions, hardware, glue, sandpaper, stain, and varnish—are included by almost all kit companies. Be sure to check, though, when ordering, because a few firms do not always furnish both stain and finishing compounds as part of the kit. Kit prices are nominally lower when these items are not included. Often you can order them separately from the kit company or buy them on your own locally.

In all the years we've worked with kits, there were only two pieces for which we needed any tool besides a hammer and screwdriver: a Queen Anne lowboy and a Chippendale block-front chest. In these instances, we used four metal bar clamps to ensure firm bonding of the wood, even distribution of pressure while the glue was drying, and true alignment. Clamps are especially useful when building the more complex kits, and hardware stores stock them at a modest price. We've also found that such tools as a hand drill, a rubber mallet, and a chisel are helpful.

Knockdown contemporary furniture requires only a screwdriver to assemble—or in some cases an Allen wrench

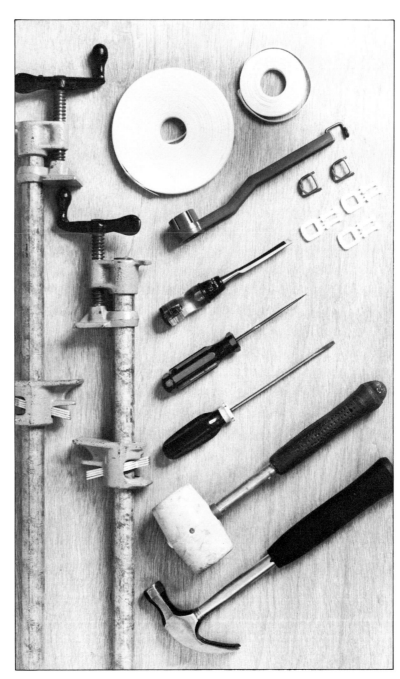

The Kit Builder's Tool Arsenal

Right, from bottom to top:

Hammer—a top priority, so make it a good, solid one. I like a rubber-grip handle.

Rubber mallet—for pounding stubborn joints together or disengaging mistakes before the glue sets; rubber head will not mar wood.

Screwdriver—regular blade will suffice.

Awl—for making starter holes for screws.

Chisel—for enlarging a tight mortise or scraping off dried glue.

Web clamps—a less cumbersome and less expensive alternative to bar clamps; use these plastic straps to tighten, clamp, or hold.

Left:

Bar clamps—useful when assembling large kits such as dressers and highboys; use to ensure good bonding while glue dries and to guarantee true alignment.

to tighten bolts; the wrench is often provided with the furniture.

FIRST STEPS

Open the box (but don't discard it yet) and remove the contents. Check the box carefully for any small envelopes, frequently used to package the hardware, that may have lodged in corners. Then compare the actual contents to the list sent by the supplier.

Read the instructions until you have a clear picture of how the pieces are assembled. Most instructions feature a clear line drawing of the assembled piece with individual parts numbered or lettered to correspond to directions given in narrative form. Don't hesitate to move the pieces around, simulating actual positions. If a piece is missing, make a note of it. Then check the wood for any damaged pieces.

Manufacturers usually include a sheet on which you can jot down oversights for return. Companies are remarkably faithful about sending out any needed replacements, usually by return mail. (If you're in a hurry, you can telephone, but companies will not accept collect calls.) We've assembled some 15 kits over the past four years, and on only one occasion were we lacking a part—two screws—which we were able to replace at negligible cost.

If in the process of examining the wood you find a small dent, apply water to the dent and allow to dry for a day. Or you may hold a steam iron over the wood and steam-mist the dent. This should raise the grain on the wood sufficiently. Bare wood, especially larger flat pieces, may warp when exposed to high humidity. If warpage has occurred, first see if the piece straightens during assembly. If not, apply water to the concave side until straight. Allow a day or two to dry.

If after examining the pieces you must put the project aside for some reason, carefully repack the contents and store the box flat in a cool, dry room (not the basement or garage). Wrap any large pieces of wood (like tabletops) in plastic wrap before putting them back into the box. This is particularly important if you order furniture during months of high humidity.

THE DRY RUN

The single most important preliminary step—besides verifying that all parts are accounted for and you understand their positioning—is to make certain

PUTTING IT ALL TOGETHER

you can comfortably, applying only *slight* pressure, make all joints together snugly. If you cannot do this without resorting to a sledge hammer, either remove the extra wood with a razor blade or, as most people do, carefully sand the joint evenly until it fits snugly. How snugly? Well, just remember once you apply the glue, the wood will swell a bit (moisture causes any bare wood to expand), and the fit will be slightly tighter than before.

It is obviously easier to shave off extra wood than to add it on, so most companies leave from a hair to a modest sliver of additional wood on a tenon or a dovetail. In the unlikely event that you find the joints of your kit fit too loosely when you first attempt a fitting, however, try applying water to see whether the wood will expand enough to ensure a good fit. Depending on where the joint occurs in the kit, it might not be critical that it fit tightly. You can glue it as usual, fill around the joint with a good wood filler, and sand it down. Or glue a thin piece of cloth or a few lengths of thread around the joint and let dry before proceeding. While photographing the Shaker rocker for the step-by-step section, we found it necessary to assemble and disassemble the chair (without gluing, of course) four

times, and the joints still fit snugly at the final gluing stage.

GLUING

Flatten the box used to ship your kit and spread it on the floor where you plan to work, in order to protect the surface from glue mess.

All kit companies include an adequate supply of glue to complete your kit. Should you run short because of a spill, buy any glue recommended for bonding wood surfaces at a hardware store. There is a special glue, called carpenter's wood glue, made for working with wood, but any glue such as Elmer's will do the job. White glue shows up well on raw wood and is preferable to beige-colored glue, which tends to blend with the unfinished wood tone, making it more difficult to tell just where and how much glue you have applied.

Be careful not to use too much glue. Today's glue is strong and bonds firmly. If the glue gushes out of the joint when fitted, you've used too much. If glue does get onto any outside wood surface, do *not* remove the excess with water. Wait until the glue has dried entirely, and carefully remove it with a razor blade or X-Acto knife.

Then sand the affected area to remove any imperfections made by the blade or glue residue.

Always be certain to read the kit manufacturer's instructions before applying glue. Never, for example, apply glue to the tenon of a chair rail; instead, apply it to the *inside* of the hole that will receive it. The reason for this is simple: glue causes the tenon to swell, frequently making it impossible to fit the tenon into the hole after gluing.

If you discover you've made an error and the glue has not yet set, use a mallet or hammer to disengage the joint. Grip the piece securely and strike firmly. Two blows should suffice. Never hammer the wood directly; place a protective wedge of wood between the hammer or mallet and the kit wood.

SANDING

In most cases, you will find the time it takes to sand, stain, and finish the furniture kit far exceeds the hours spent on assembly.

Once you've carefully glued the pieces together, you'll probably be eager to finish your kit. But don't rush through the remaining steps. Your finished piece of furniture will only look

as good as the effort you make in sanding it.

The more time you set aside to sand carefully and steadily, the better prepared the surface of the wood will be to absorb the stain evenly and to take on a fine patina with repeated coats of a finishing compound.

The two cardinal rules of sanding are not to use flint sandpaper and not to sand across the grain. Flint paper is inexpensive to buy but tends to lose grit particles, which can then mar the surface being sanded. As for sanding with the grain, one way to simplify the task is to position the piece you're working on so that the wood grain runs with your body, not opposite it.

Begin sanding your piece with #120 or #150 grit paper (depending on how rough the wood is), then move on to #180. The higher the number, the finer the tooth on the paper. The #320-grade sandpaper is very fine and should only be used during the final sanding. You will have more control (and be able to bear down harder) when you sand if you wrap the paper around a piece of hard wood.

Sand all areas equally. If possible, don't allow more than 24 hours to pass between the final sanding and applying the finish, because raw wood is more vulnerable to moisture from the air and to dents.

To reach difficult spots (between spindles, for instance) cut a long, thin piece of sandpaper and move it back and forth like a shoeshine cloth. Sand around spindles by folding a piece of sandpaper and twisting the paper and turning the spindle at the same time. Also fold paper to sand between thin edges of molding.

If you want to give a smooth-as-glass feel to a flat surface such as a tabletop, begin by moistening the entire top with a damp cloth. Allow the wood to dry, then resand with #320 grit paper wrapped around a hard sanding block. Repeat this moistening-sanding process (called feathering the grain) until the wood grain no longer rises on the wood. Spectacularly smooth results are guaranteed with this bit of extra effort.

If once your sanding is complete you accidentally nick the wood surface, there are a number of ways to repair it. One way is to try to steam it out, using the method described on page 121. Another approach that's frequently recommended is to buy stick shellac, which comes in a wide range of colors to match the stain you plan to use. Melt the shellac into the imperfection and let

it cool. The shellac hardens almost immediately, and you can then sand the piece level and proceed with staining.

STAINING

Most kit companies that include stain with their kits offer a variety of colors to choose from. If you'd like to try out the color before staining the whole kit, either apply it to a scrap of the same kind of wood or wipe a bit on the underside of the kit. You can always use commercially available stains if you decide that you want a different color.

Once you've decided on a color, vacuum the entire piece and then wipe it with a tack cloth (available at hardware stores) to remove the last traces of grit. Brush or wipe on the stain in small amounts on small areas. Apply carefully and evenly, avoiding drips that may leave lasting marks. If you're using paste stain, don't bear down hard while applying or the tone will be uneven. Always stain hard-to-reach places first, such as chair bottoms and rungs. Keep a supply of cotton swabs or an artist's brush on hand for getting stain into tight areas. When staining drawers, take them out of the cabinet and stand them on end, with the drawer front facing up; you'll get a more consistent tone this way.

If your kit requires another coat of stain to deepen the color, allow from 3 to 4 hours drying time between coats. If you feel rough spots between applications, rub lightly with 4/0 (#0000) steel wool.

End grains of wood (edges of tabletops and drawers) tend to stain darker than the rest of the wood. To avoid this, apply a little paste varnish along with paste stain (if that's what you're using) to dilute the tone. Or, if you're using liquid stain, apply a thin coat of shellac or linseed oil to seal the wood, thus preventing it from absorbing too much stain. Let dry before staining.

If you choose to buy your own stain, there are many choices available today. My favorite stain for finishing our Colonial kits is ''Light Oak,'' made by Pratt & Lambert, a warm ocher-honey tone that darkens nicely with age. For our kitchen cabinets, I mixed a tiny dollop of burnt umber oil pigment with the light oak, but for all the bedroom

furniture I applied the stain straight from the can after first sealing the pine so that it wouldn't soak up gallons of stain. (Any soft and porous wood ideally should be sealed before staining— although it's not absolutely necessary.)

Of the seven major kinds of stains— penetrating oil, varnish, wax, water, chemical, alcohol, and pigment oil— only the first three are sold ready-to-use at hardware and paint stores. The others are not used as widely by the general public, primarily because they must be mixed and some care must be exercised in their application. You don't have to be a professional, however, to experiment with these stains. In fact, if you're choosy about your colors and have been disappointed with commercial preparations in the past, you might try mixing your own batch of stain.

The following chart lists the seven basic stains and briefly points out their advantages and disadvantages, along with any required mixing formulas.

Of all the books on staining and finishing that I consulted during the preparation of this section, by far the most useful and definitive proved to be Wood: Finishing and Refinishing *by S. W. Gibbia (see Additional Reading).*

PUTTING IT ALL TOGETHER

Stain	Basis	Preparation	Pros	Cons	Tips
Penetrating oil stain	*Coal-tar dyes dissolved in naphtha, benzine, or turpentine.*	*Sold ready to use.*	*Soaks into wood quickly; gives a clear, transparent look, allowing wood grain to show through. Colors remain consistent in lines manufactured by reliable companies. Widely available in paint and hardware stores.*	*Limited shades available. Because of oil base, it takes at least a day to dry. You sometimes cannot apply a varnish finish directly over oil stains because oil may seep through, muddying the tone; it may be necessary to seal first with thinned shellac. (Check varnish label to be sure.)*	*To eliminate overlap marks while applying stain, always brush with the wood grain from left to right in long, even strokes. Try to get across the length with one brushful. Wipe off excess with a clean cloth, again moving with the grain. To prevent spontaneous combustion, do not allow oily rags to pile up in work area—either soak in water or destroy.*
Wax stain	*Penetrating oil stain mixed with wax and a drying agent.*	*Sold ready to use.*	*Easy to apply; does not raise grain; many colors available. Gives a soft, hand-rubbed look. Beyond a final coat of paste finishing wax, no other finishing compound is necessary. White shellac may be used to give a protective coating.*	*Not recommended where a hard, shiny finish is desired.*	*Minwax makes a line of wax stains that is widely available in hardware and paint stores.*
Pigment oil stain	*Oil colors mixed with linseed oil, turpentine, and fast-drying varnish (japan drier).*	*For 1 pint of stain, mix: 1/4 pound oil color of choice (oil pigments are sold in pint containers as well as tubes), 1 cup turpentine or benzine, 3 ounces boiled linseed oil, 1/4 ounce japan drier. Pour turpentine or benzine into a metal or glass container; add color, linseed oil, and the drier. Mix well. Keep container sealed between uses.*	*Easy to apply evenly. Wide range of colors possible.*	*Does not penetrate deeply; slightly translucent rather than fully transparent; fades when exposed to sunlight over time. Requires 24 hours to dry. May require a thin coat of shellac before varnish can be applied; check varnish label to be sure.*	*To achieve an antiqued look, apply a dark pigment oil stain over a light-finished surface. Wipe off carefully. You'll get a gently contrasting color.*

Stain	Basis	Preparation	Pros	Cons	Tips
Water stain	*Coal-tar or vegetable dyes (anilines) dissolved in water.*	*Buy water-soluble dye in the color of your choice at paint stores. Boil a quart of water and pour it into a metal container. Add 1 ounce of the powder. Let cool and use.*	*Gives deep, permanent penetration; won't fade in sunlight. Dries in a few hours. Inexpensive to make; you can stain a major piece of furniture for about $0.50. Dyes give the largest variety of vivid colors of any stain.*	*Bare wood surface must be prepared to receive stain by wetting wood with water, letting dry, and then sanding with 3/0 garnet paper—otherwise water stain will raise grain of wood. Surface streaking common. Practice brush strokes for best results.*	*Do not attempt to use water stains on old pieces of furniture from which other stains and finishes have been removed—the stain won't penetrate the wood.*
Chemical stain	*Acid or alkaline substances (such as lye, sal soda, or vinegar) dissolved in warm water.*	*Add 2 ounces chemical to 1 quart of water.*	*Inexpensive to prepare, and ingredients are available in most households. Permanently staining.*	*Must prepare wood as with water stains—wetting and sanding. Rubber gloves should be worn because chemicals are caustic. Stains must be tested first on piece of scrap wood to see what color will be achieved.*	*To give pine a wonderfully grayed and weathered look, take 1 pint of white vinegar in which nails have been soaked overnight and apply liquid to raw wood.* *Store chemical stains in glass containers.*
Varnish stain	*Penetrating oil stain mixed with varnish.*	*Sold ready to use.*	*Practical and fast; combines stain with protective finish. Especially useful on interior surfaces (drawers, cabinets, etc.).*	*Expensive. Does not penetrate surface; can look dull as a result. Not appropriate where a fine finish is desired.*	*You can mix your own varnish stain by combining varnish and oil stain.*
Alcohol stain	*Alcohol-soluble powder dissolved in alcohol.*	*For most stains, dissolve 1/2 ounce of alcohol-soluble powder in 1 quart of alcohol.*	*Will not raise grain, so wetting and sanding step unnecessary. Dries at once on raw wood. Can change color of already finished furniture, since alcohol stain will penetrate varnish or shellac.*	*Virtually impossible to stain a large surface such as a tabletop without streaking because stain dries on contact. Will fade in time when exposed to sunlight; penetration not as deep as with water stains.*	*Use a sprayer to apply alcohol stain to larger pieces to eliminate chances of streaking.*

PUTTING IT ALL TOGETHER

FINISHING

Staining alone will not protect your furniture. It's important to finish your kit further to protect the wood from dirt, heat, and moisture and to bring out the qualities and colors inherent in the wood. The top few thousandths of an inch—actually all the viewer sees—is the sliver that must hold up under considerable wear and tear, especially on surfaces such as tabletops.

Finishes either penetrate the wood or form a film on top of it. Oils afford some protection to surfaces, but their biggest selling point is the way they soak into the wood and enhance, in a natural-looking way, the tactile quality of the furniture. Varnish and lacquer, on the other hand, give maximum protection to surfaces, but when you touch a table that has been varnished, you're not touching the wood but the surface film on top.

It's important to remember that not all furniture needs the same kind or amount of protection. One finish should not be applied to every piece, nor should all parts of the same piece necessarily receive the same number of finishing coats. The penetrating oil finish that protects and enhances a butcher block table will look dull on an elegant Queen Anne chair, where the gleam of a semigloss varnish is more in character. Similarly, the extra coat of finish that you add to a dresser or tabletop isn't necessary on drawers and legs, which don't get the same wear.

Whether you opt for a penetrating finish that will bring out the natural beauty of the wood or a hard protective film, the following chart should help make your choice easier.

Finish	Basis	Application	Clean-up	Pros	Cons	Tips
Polyurethane varnish	Clear, oil-modified urethane.	Brush or spray. Surface can be rubbed with 3/0 steel wool 3 hours after applying varnish. Several coats are recommended.	Mineral spirits or turpentine.	Gives a tough surface on both interior and exterior woods. Resistant to water, heat, acid, grease, and alcohol. Dries in 1 hour.	Will scorch when subjected to high heat. Looks more artificial than other finishes; nicks and scratches easily.	Products such as Varsol are preferable to turpentine for thinning. Do not apply polyurethane varnish over shellac or lacquer finishes; it will not adhere.

Finish	Basis	Application	Clean-up	Pros	Cons	Tips
Fast-drying varnish	*Synthetic resins, China wood oil or tung oil, thinners.*	*Stir, do not shake, container. Using a flat 2-inch or 3-inch brush, apply three thin, even coats to surface free of oil and dirt; sand dried surface between coats with 4/0 steel wool and wipe off dust with tack cloth (available at hardware stores). Brush on final coat slightly thicker. Let piece dry in dust-free room. Apply when temperature is between 70 and 80 degrees, but not on humid days.*	*Mineral spirits or turpentine.*	*Tougher than either shellac or lacquer; gives a clear, resilient finish that will stand up to water, heat, and alcohol. Flows on easily, gives wood excellent body, is transparent, and will not alter color of wood or stain.*	*Minimum drying time between coats is 4 hours. To get good results, you must work under dust-free conditions.*	
Boiled linseed oil	*Drying oil obtained from flaxseed.*	*The old-fashioned method is to wipe on the oil and rub and rub until the excess is removed. Do this once a day for 7 days, once a week for 30 days, once a month for a year, and then once a year thereafter. Some recommend a mixture of 1 pint linseed oil, 1 ounce burnt sienna oil pigment, and 2 tablespoons japan drier. Heat in a double boiler.*	*Turpentine.*	*Final finish is durable and fairly resistant to water, heat, and scratches. Easy to apply and touch up.*	*Surfaces can get sticky (and attract dust), especially during humid weather. Not suggested for use on chairs or on cherry or walnut (tends to turn walnut black). Long application time; upkeep necessary.*	

PUTTING IT ALL TOGETHER

Finish	Basis	Application	Clean-up	Pros	Cons	Tips
Penetrating oil sealers	*Resins with driers added.*	*Brush or wipe on with a rag. Let first coat penetrate for 15 to 30 minutes, then wipe off excess. Let harden (check label for time required), then apply second coat in same manner. Once second coat has hardened, wax may be applied for shine.*	*Paint thinner.*	*Resembles a hand-rubbed linseed oil finish but takes much less work. Finish is durable, fairly resistant to water, heat, and scratches, and easy to apply and touch up. Little upkeep necessary. Available in various shades as well as in clear; staining and finishing can thus be done in one step.*	*Not appropriate where a high-gloss finish is desired.*	*Brand-name sealers to consider include Watco Danish Oil and Minwax Antique Oil.*
Tung oil	*Aromatic natural drying oil from the nuts of the tung tree.*	*Tung oil is available both thinned and unthinned. The thinned version is easier to apply and faster-drying. Apply with rag or brush. Wipe off excess after oil soaks into wood. Allow 1 to 10 minutes soaking time, depending on weather. Two or three coats are recommended; let each dry for at least an hour. After final coat has dried for a day, burnish with 4/0 steel wool to even out sheen.*	*Mineral spirits or lacquer thinner.*	*Easy to apply; dries quickly; emphasizes grain and natural qualities of wood. Gives a better sheen than other oil finishes. Water and solvent resistant.*	*Somewhat expensive. Not appropriate where a high-gloss finish is desired.*	*Use lemon oil to clean and shine tung oil finishes. To keep leftover tung oil longer, keep container full by dropping pebbles into can; otherwise oil will congeal.*

Finish	Basis	Application	Clean-up	Pros	Cons	Tips
Shellac	Dried resin secretion (lac) from a Far Eastern scale insect dissolved in alcohol.	When using a brush, work fast and apply shellac in long strokes that don't overlap; if using a spray gun, be careful to maintain an even distance from the piece at all times; if using a pad, make sure it's lint-free and dampen it first in alcohol. All shellacked surfaces (except those rubbed with a pad) can be burnished to a smooth, velvety finish if rubbed with steel wool.	Alcohol.	Fast-drying, protects well, lasts. Dries dustproof very quickly. Easy to touch up; no maintenance.	Not waterproof or heatproof; especially vulnerable to alcohol. Will turn white outdoors. Does not store well over 6 months (keep in glass containers, not metal ones).	White shellac (with a bleaching agent added) will not measurably alter the color of wood surfaces. Shellac's natural color is orange; use orange shellac only on dark-stained surfaces such as mahogany.
Wood lacquer	Resins, nitrocellulose, solvents, softeners, thinners.	Spray gun is best, but not for the inexperienced; special brushing lacquers are also available. You must thin with lacquer thinner, but be careful; the more thinner you use, the faster the lacquer dries and the harder it is to work.	Lacquer thinner (buy same brand as the lacquer you're using). Buy twice as much thinner as lacquer.	Fastest-drying finish ever developed, so you can apply several coats on the same day. Resists heat; withstands moisture. Some lacquers are alcohol-proof. Gives wood a natural, transparent surface and doesn't affect color of stained wood.	Because it dries so quickly, lacquer is difficult to apply with a brush. Requires practice because it tends to pull; you cannot work it as you do varnish. Before using lacquer over an oil-based stain, seal piece with shellac. Toxic and highly explosive.	Lacquer can be purchased in aerosol cans, which are good for small jobs or touch-up work. Don't get too close when spraying or the lacquer will run.

PUTTING IT ALL TOGETHER

WAXING

Once you've stained and finished your kit, the final (and very important) step is to apply a good grade of wax. Wax will bring out the wood's luster, protect the surface from abrasions, and cut down on maintenance.

You can buy wax in either paste or liquid form. I strongly recommend the paste form. All paste waxes contain varying amounts of carnauba wax; the more carnauba the harder the film will be and the greater the luster. Carnauba wax comes in a colorless white form or in dark brown for darker furniture such as mahogany.

Paste wax can be applied with a cloth (a ball of cheesecloth is best) or, for an even smoother surface, with either 2/0 or 3/0 (#00 or #000) steel wool. Buff *lightly*. There will be no gummy film or fingerprints. Apply wax in thin coats and do not overwax your piece. Twice-a-year waxing with buffing in between should suffice.

PAINTING WOOD

Many of the pieces produced in the colonies in the seventeenth century were either painted or stained with a bright color. In some cases they were further decorated with painted designs. Cabinetmakers from Spain, Germany, and Scandinavia painted much of their furniture, especially chests and cupboards. Their motifs—hearts, tulips, six-pointed stars, unicorns, and flowers of all kinds—had special symbolic meaning.

Some furniture historians believe that woodworkers painted pieces that were built out of several different woods as a way of concealing this fact. Others feel that the use of paint was an aesthetic decision, a way of showing off the lovely Colonial paints.

Whatever the reason, painting wood is a very useful way of finishing furniture. Paint hides defects in wood, and painted pieces are easier to maintain because their surfaces can be cleaned with soap and water. And paint is easy to apply—simply do hard-to-reach places first, and tops and seats last.

Colonial cabinetmakers used milk-based paints, which subsequent generations have found to be extraordinarily long lasting (most chemical paint removers won't budge them!). Today, Turco Coatings, Inc. (Wheatland & Mellon Streets, Phoenixville, PA 19460) manufactures milk-based paints, as does The Old-Fashioned Milk Paint Co. (P.O. Box 222HB, Groton, MA 01450). If you'd like to mix your own batch, try this recipe by Jon W. Arno published in *Fine Woodworking* magazine:

Reconstitute instant nonfat dry milk, using just enough hot water to dissolve the milk into a thick, smooth syrup. Add pigment in small increments and mix thoroughly. Vary the opacity and color by adding either more hot water or pigment, testing the mixture from time to time on a piece of scrap. Apply to raw wood with a brush or rag while the paint is still warm. When dry, it will have an almost dead flat finish much like latex wall paint, but with a certain translucence all its own. For an antique look, use full-strength milk paint and rub it with a damp cloth as it dries: the opacity of the paint in the corners and crevices will contrast with the lighter finish of the rubbed surface.

The pigments that produce colors like those seen in books and museums are the earth colors: burnt sienna, Venetian red and Indian red. The latter is best, but hard to find. Acrylic paints also work, and the choice of colors there is mindboggling.

Seal with a coat of varnish or shellac rubbed down to a satin finish, which will protect the paint and mask its odor at the same time.

For those who prefer to let the wood grain show through, one of the best paint stains on the market is Watco's 5-minute transparent stains. The line includes nine colors that can be mixed, and lighter shades can be obtained by using #8 stain reducer. These stains do not raise the grain of the wood.

For an extremely opaque finish, the best paint to use is an enamel with an alkyd-resin base. Do not use a latex-base paint. The water in these paints will raise the grain of the wood, making it rough, and the paint will penetrate the wood to such an extent that removal in the future will be all but impossible.

Before applying the first coat, wet the surface and feather the grain as described on page 124. Seal pine first with white shellac sealer to prevent knots from bleeding through the paint. The first coat should be an undercoat, or primer. Let dry at least one day. Smooth lightly with an extra-fine sandpaper wrapped around a wood block. Apply enamel, either semiglossy or glossy. Let dry, then sand surface roughly so it will be receptive to a final coat of paint.

To give a low-luster finish to your kit after painting, rub with pumice powder

Cohasset Colonials' stenciling kit ($14.00) makes it possible to duplicate the primitive painted designs often found on Colonial furniture. The blanket chest is $139.00.

PUTTING IT ALL TOGETHER

and oil. If you want to give an antiqued look, buy a glazing liquid, available in paint or art stores, and apply as directed. If you want to imitate wormholes on the surface, dip an old toothbrush in paint, bend back the bristles with your fingers, and spray the paint over the desired area. You can get other special effects by crumpling newspaper and using it to make coarse patterns on still-wet glaze.

Special effects are not new in furniture history. An 1835 pine box found in Maine had been painted and then smoked with a candle flame to produce a shadowy image on the box. Stenciling, which was first introduced as a way to imitate gilt decorating, later found its way to the mass market in the form of the popular Hitchcock chair, which was heavily stenciled. The chairs, prized by collectors today, sold for $1.50 in the 1820s and were hawked by peddlers throughout the East.

Cohasset Colonials sells stencil kits with which you can paint an eagle on a chest or floral designs on the crest rail of a turned ladderback chair.

RUSHING SEATS

Rush seats date back to Egyptian times when rushes were gathered by stream banks and marshes from plants such as bulrushes and cattails. Nowadays, rush fibers used to weave seats are made of machine-twisted paper.

Before rushing seats, dampen the rush material by plunging it into water and removing it immediately. Then weave the seat. As it dries it will shrink slightly, making a tauter seat. Do not soak the rush material; it will not hold up.

Be careful not to overlap the strands at the corners. The strands should fit snugly where they go over the rails. To ensure this, place a block of wood at the base of the fiber and pound with a hammer or mallet *every time you complete a new row*. This action will also keep the angles straight.

Once the seat is finished, apply at least three coats of a fine-grade varnish. The varnish will hold the strands in place and make the seat more durable and attractive. When you've applied enough varnish there will be no dull areas left on the fibers.

Rushing is far more demanding an art than weaving tapes. Unless you're up for a challenge, or have rushing experience, be prepared for sore hands and, perhaps, less-than-perfect results.

LIVING WITH WOOD

I always think of lumbered wood as still possessing some of the qualities of the live tree. Wood furniture changes; it expands, contracts, and even cracks under certain conditions. Cracks and gaps found in antique pieces probably occurred within a couple of years after construction when the wood was young. Stain colors change; finishes mellow. It's all part of the life process of wood furniture.

If during low humidity you find a crack in your kit—or any piece of furniture for that matter—apply a little Fil-Stik (available at hardware stores) to the crack. Do not use glue. When the air becomes moister, the crack will swell and close, pushing out the Fil-Stik.

No two pieces of wood are alike. So if the grain of the tabletop in your kit does not match exactly, don't despair. If you find a wormhole, consider yourself lucky. Some people request wormholes! Mass-produced furniture has a monotonously consistent grain pattern, especially noticeable in vinyl veneers, which possess no warmth or individuality.

Nearly all established kit companies today use solid woods in their kits. You should, however, check individual catalogs closely. If the wood used is not solid, the manufacturer will so state.

If your piece of solid wood should break at any time, just glue it together and apply pressure while it is drying, with a web or bar clamp. That's another plus in working with quality solid woods.

The photographs that follow indicate step-by-step assemblies of three different kits (a canopy bed, a Shaker rocker, and a Chippendale chest) in far greater detail than you're likely to encounter in kit instructions. Whether or not you intend to assemble any of these particular kits, it's a good idea to review the photographs carefully. That way you'll become familiar with many of the most common joints and procedures used in building kits: applying glue to joints, pounding a tenon into a mortise, assembling a drawer. The photographs should also serve to nurture confidence in future kit builders; as you'll see, kit building is *not* a herculean task.

THREE KITS STEP-BY-STEP

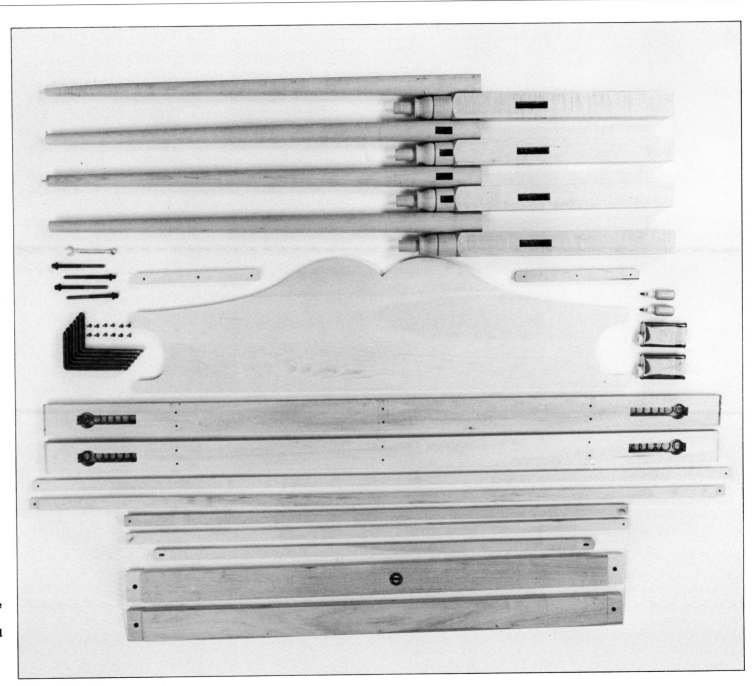

The 20 pieces of the canopy bed, plus hardware, glue, and stain, as they are unpacked from the shipping carton.

STEP-BY-STEP BED

1. After applying glue to the walls of the deep mortises in the tapered posts, head legs, and headboard mortises, insert the headboard and the crossrail into the matching mortises. Use a hammer or mallet and block of wood to make insertion easier, as pictured.

2. Follow same procedure in inserting the bottom crossrail into the foot legs. The head and foot sections of your bed are now complete.

3. To attach side rails to head and foot legs, insert bolts in the nuts and tighten with a wrench (provided) until the side shoulders are against the legs. *No glue should be applied to these joints.*

4. Fasten metal hangers to side rails with flathead screws. Make certain you attach the hanger with the extra hole in the center of bed, to accommodate the slat that will span the width of bed in the middle. This slat will support the springs and mattress.

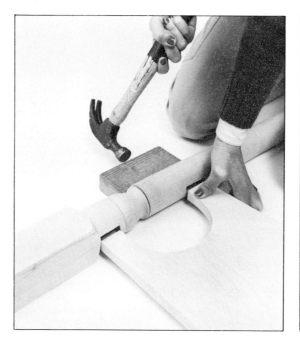
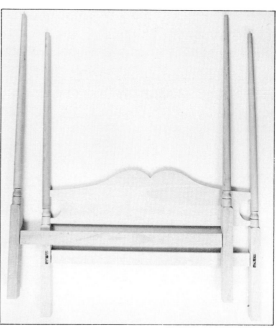
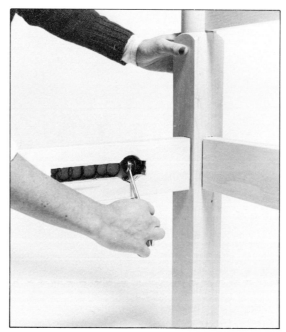

5. The four sections of the canopy frame simply slip over the pins at the top of the tapered posts. No glue is necessary. Your canopy bed frame will now look like this, ready for staining and finishing.

6. The finished product.

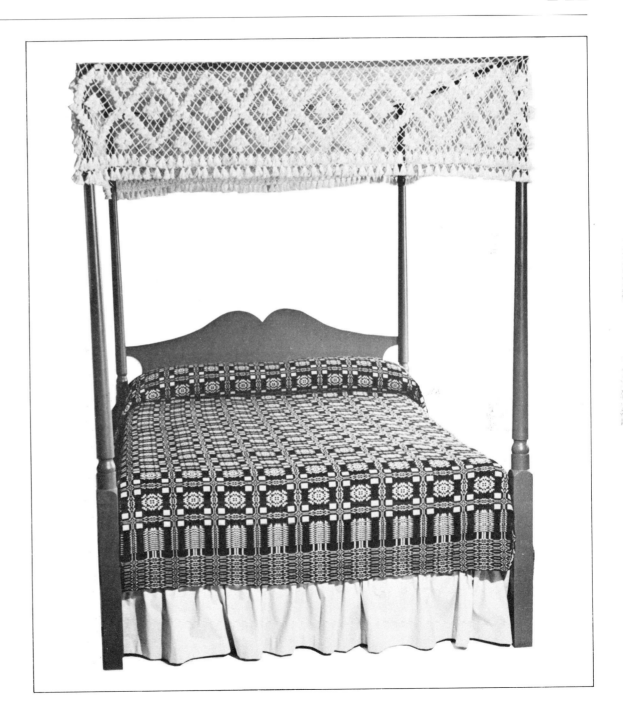

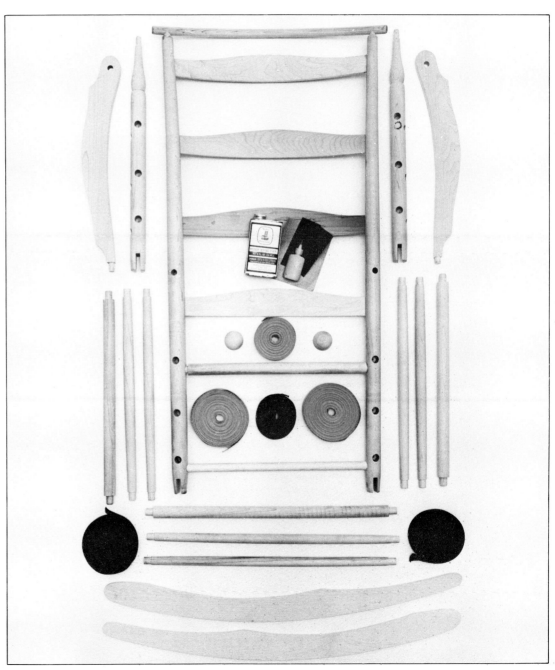

The unassembled rocker as removed from the shipping container.

STEP-BY-STEP ROCKER

1. Check rails for proper fit. Then apply glue sparingly with a toothpick to the *sides of the holes* that will receive the front rails.

2. Insert rails, then rest assembly on its side on top of a folded towel. Pound with a hammer along the length of the posts until the rail ends will go no farther, using a strip of soft wood between the post and the hammer to protect the chair.

3. Glue and assemble side rails, then add arms. Your chair should now consist of two sections. Glue and join the front unit to the preassembled back.

4. Before glue sets, check that all four legs sit evenly on a flat surface. If the chair wobbles, bounce the frame *lightly* on the leg that appears to be too long. Then invert chair and check the diagonal distance between the legs. If they're not equal, tie a rope around the longer diagonal, and twist with a stick of wood until the distances even out.

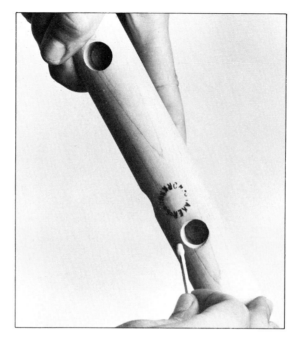

5. Position the rockers, then make a hole in the legs to receive the screws, using a hand drill with a 1/8-inch bit, a finishing nail, or an awl (pictured) to make the hole. Apply a little soap to screw threads to facilitate entry into the wood.

6. Your chair is now ready to be finished. After sanding away rough spots and any glue residue, wipe off dust and apply stain to small sections at a time, using two cotton socks over the hand as an applicator. Wipe off excess and let dry. Then apply another coat to deepen color, or proceed directly to finishing.

7. After finish has dried thoroughly, chair seat may be woven; complete instructions come with the kit. If you have never woven a seat before, allow 3 to 4 hours. The beige tape here, called the *warp*, is used to cover the seat from front to back. The brown tape, or *woof*, is then woven through the warp. Pull the tapes firmly, and be sure to weave the bottom of the seat as well.

8. The finished rocker ready for years of service.

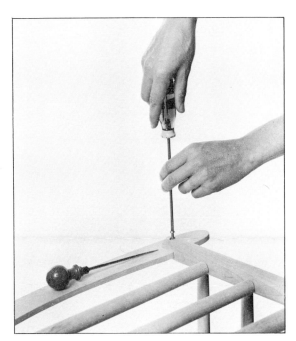
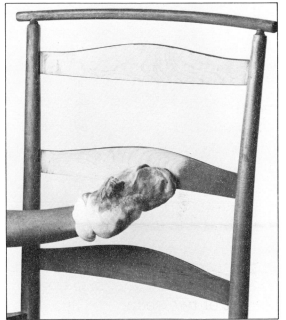

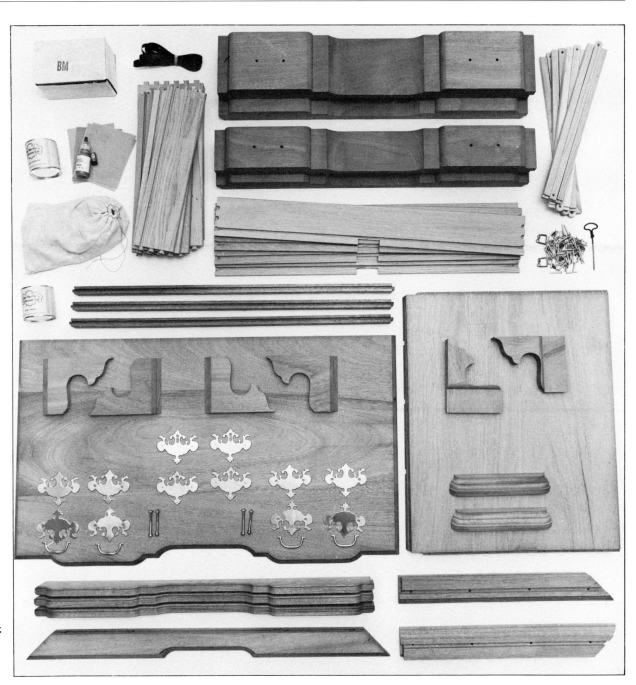

Unassembled blockfront chest ingredients, arranged and ready to be assembled.

STEP-BY-STEP CHEST

1. Drawer components before gluing; note that each of the four drawers is a different size. Apply glue *only* to the dovetail joints of the drawer frame; once the sides are attached to the front, the drawer bottom slides easily into place and should not be glued. (That way it can expand and contract with changes in humidity, making the drawer easier to maneuver.) Glue back of drawer to sides.

2. Once the four sides and bottom of the drawer are in place, attach the grooved drawer guide with screws and glue, and glue the rub blocks in place—one on each side and two each on the front and back. Complete one drawer at a time, and allow at least 2 hours for each to dry completely.

3. Attach the front base rail to the left and right side base rails using glue and clamp nails. Hammer the nails into the groove, sharp edge down.

4. Attach the base overlay to the base using a small amount of glue and the screws provided.

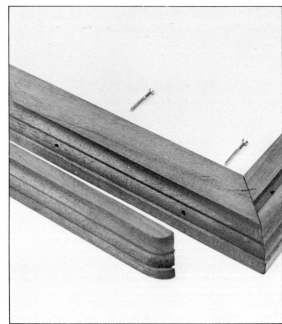

5. Slide the drawer base bottom in from the back.

6. Secure the sides to the base using a small amount of glue and the screws provided.

7. Secure the sides to the top using a small amount of glue and the screws provided.

8. Glue the front dust-divider rails to the sides, putting glue on the mortise, not on the tenon.

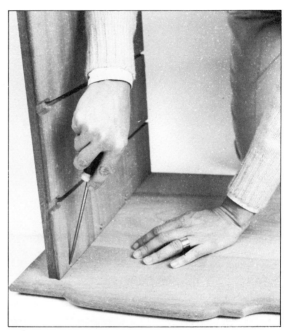
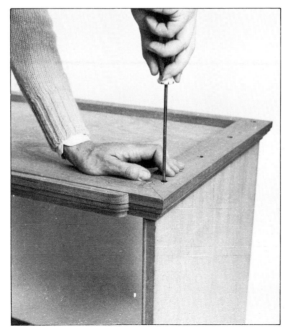

STEP-BY-STEP CHEST

9. After the glue on the front dust-divider rails has dried for 3 to 4 hours, insert the dust-divider side rails.

10. Slide the plywood dust dividers into the grooves.

11. Glue the dust-divider back rails into place.

12. Assemble the legs with glue and the clamp nails.

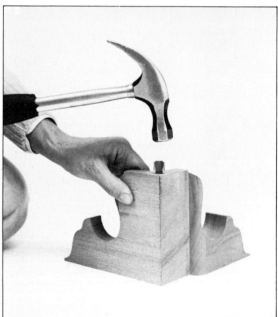

13. Attach the cleats to the legs, using glue and the screws.

14. Center, glue, and screw the legs on the corners 1/16 inch from the edges of the cabinet.

15. Screw the back end of the guide to the back dust-panel rail.

16. Remove the drawers and attach the front of the guide with screws at the center of the front divider rail.

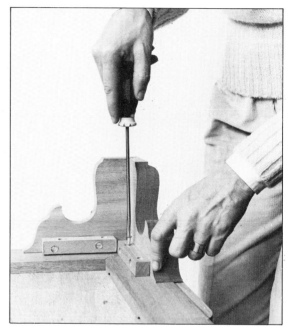

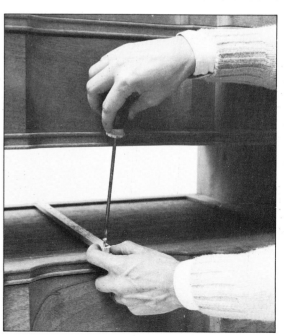

STEP-BY-STEP CHEST

17. Attach the large back panel to the lower portion of the cabinet with the wire nails and glue.

18. Fully assembled, ready to be stained and finished. After finishing, attach the brass hardware.

19. The final result, a chest to be proud of for years to come.

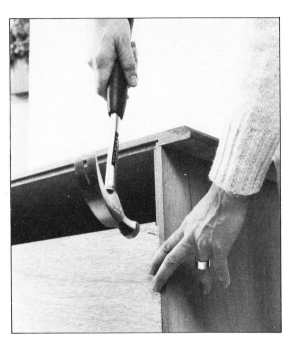

DIRECTORY OF MANUFACTURERS & RETAILERS

COMPANY/ADDRESS	CATALOG PRICE	AVAILABILITY
American Forest Products Co. 2740 Hyde Street San Francisco, CA 94119	—	*Nationwide—J.C. Penney catalog, Montgomery Ward catalog; New England—Century Lumber; New Jersey—Jefferson Ward Stores; Mid-Atlantic—Rickel Home Centers; California—Pay 'N Save Home Centers.*
The Bartley Collection, Ltd. 747 Oakwood Avenue Lake Forest, IL 60045	$1.00	*Mail order; Lake Forest showroom open Monday to Saturday 10 to 5; phone charge mail orders (800) 228-2606.*
Enrico Bartolini Designs Narrows Center, Route 11 Kingston, PA 18704	—	*Retail only: New York City—Sachs, Macy's; Boston—Jordan Marsh; San Antonio—Joskes; Florida—Robinsons.*
Bow House, Inc. Box 62 Bolton, MA 01740	$4.00	*Mail order; for model home directions call (617) 779-6464 or write.*
J&D Brauner/Butcher Block 298 Bowery New York, NY 10012 1735 N. Ashland Avenue Chicago, IL 60622 11677 Santa Monica Boulevard Los Angeles, CA 90025	$1.00	*Retail stores: New York—Long Island City, New York City, Scarsdale; Paramus, New Jersey; Chicago; Milwaukee; Los Angeles. Mail and phone orders accepted.*
Carroll Industries Conway, NH 03818	—	*Available at many lumberyards, hardware stores, and home supply centers.*

DIRECTORY OF MANUFACTURERS & RETAILERS

COMPANY/ADDRESS	CATALOG PRICE	AVAILABILITY
Cohasset Colonials 552EX Ship Street Cohasset, MA 02025	$1.00	*Mail order: Cohasset showroom open Monday to Saturday 9 to 4:30.*
Conran's 145 Huguenot Street New Rochelle, NY 10801	$3.50	*Retail stores: New York—New York City, New Rochelle, Manhasset; New Jersey—Hackensack; Washington, D.C.; Virginia—Fairfax County; mail order to New Rochelle address.*
Country Rag Rugs 33 North Street Dalton, MA 01226	$1.00	*Mail order.*
Craft Products Company 2200 Dean Street St. Charles, IL 60174	$1.50	*Mail order.*
Cutter Furniture Corporation P.O. Box 36 Blue Mounds, WI 53517	—	*Mail order: Kache Co., Box 215, Mt. Horet, WI 53572; retail: Pier I stores nationwide; West Coast—Akron Stores; Chicago—Carson, Pirie, Scott; East Coast—Macy's.*
Design-kit Main Street Bloomingburg, NY 12921	Free	*Mail order.*

COMPANY/ADDRESS	CATALOG PRICE	AVAILABILITY
The Door Store 1 Park Avenue New York, NY 10016	Free	*Five retail stores in New York City and by mail.*
Richard Ehrlich/Wedgelock Furniture Box 14587 Austin, TX 78761	Free	*Retail at Houston store, 1705 S. Post Oak Road, and by mail.*
Fred Ellis and Sons, Inc. P.O. Box 536 Essex, MA 01929	$1.00	*Mail order.*
Emperor Clock Company Emperor Industrial Park Fairhope, AL 36532	Free	*Mail order.*
Green Mountain Homes Royalton, VT 05068	$4.50	*Mail order.*
The Hardwood Craftsman, Ltd. 121 Schelter Ave. Prairie View, IL 60069	Free	*Mail order; charge phone orders only; call (800) 331-1750, operator 65.*

DIRECTORY OF MANUFACTURERS & RETAILERS

COMPANY/ADDRESS	CATALOG PRICE	AVAILABILITY
Heath Craft Woodworks, a division of Heath Company Benton Harbor, MI 49022	Free	*Mail order; charge phone orders only; call (800) 253-0570. Furniture available at 56 locations in U.S. at Heathkit Electronic Centers.*
Heritage Designs P.O. Box 103 410 N. Maple Monticello, IA 52310	Free	*Mail order.*
Frank Hubbard, Inc. 144 Moody Street, Bldg. 1 Waltham, MA 02154	$1.00	*Mail order.*
Imp 808 Garfield Avenue Jersey City, NJ 07305	—	*Retail only: New York City—Macy's, Conran's; Boston—Jordan Marsh; Texas—Joskes, Foleys; Florida—Jordan Marsh; California—Breuners; Illinois/California—Wickes Furniture Company.*
Jensen-Lewis 89 Seventh Avenue New York, NY 10011	$1.00	*Charge phone orders accepted; call (212) 929-4675.*
Justus Homes P.O. Box 98300 Tacoma, WA 98499	$5.00	*Mail order.*

COMPANY/ADDRESS	CATALOG PRICE	AVAILABILITY
Lord & Burnham Box 4050 Hicksville, NY 11802	$2.00	*Mail order.*
Mason & Sullivan Dept. 4515 586 Higgins Crowell Road West Yarmouth, MA 02673	Free	*Mail order; Osterville showroom open Monday to Saturday 9 to 5, Saturday 9 to 2.*
Moultrie Manufacturing Co. P.O. Drawer 1179 Moultrie, GA 31768	$1.00	*Mail order.*
Northern Homes, Inc. 10 LaCrosse Street Hudson Falls, NY 12839	$5.00	*Mail order.*
Outer Banks Pine Products P.O. Box 9003 Lester, PA 19113	$0.25	*Mail order.*
Peerless Rattan P.O. Box 8 Towaco, NJ 07082	Free	*Mail order.*

DIRECTORY OF MANUFACTURERS & RETAILERS

COMPANY/ADDRESS	CATALOG PRICE	AVAILABILITY
Real Log Homes **National Information Center** **Box 202** **Hartland, VT 05048**	$5.00	*Mail order.*
Shaker Workshops **P.O. Box 1028** **Concord, MA 01742**	$0.50	*Mail order; showroom in Arlington, Massachusetts, on Mill Lane, open Monday to Saturday 10 to 5.*
Western Reserve Antique Furniture Kit **Box 206A** **Bath, OH 44210**	$1.00	*Mail order and gift shop of Shaker Historical Society, Shaker Heights, Ohio.*
Westwood Clocks 'N Kits **3210 Airport Way** **Long Beach, CA 90806**	—	*Mail order.*
Woodcraft Supply Corp. **313 Montvale Avenue** **Woburn, MA 01888**	$1.00	*Mail order; charge mail orders only; call (800) 225-1153; Woburn store hours Monday to Saturday 9 to 6 (Thursday to 9).*

COMPANY/ADDRESS	CATALOG PRICE	AVAILABILITY
Woodcutter Company *See* **Cutter Furniture Corporation**		
Woodworks Ltd. P.O. Box 221 Beverly, WV 26253	$1.00	*Mail order; call (800) 327-9009, extension 962, for phone orders; retail: Washington, D.C.—Scan; Philadelphia—Scandia House; Pittsburgh—Studio Shop; Chicago area—Scandinavian Design; Charlottesville, N.C., and Coral Gables, Fla.—Door Store.*
Yield House Dept. 5800 North Conway, NH 03860	$1.00	*Mail order; 8 New England retail locations; for charge orders and store locations, call (800) 555-1212 and ask for toll free number for your area.*
Zimmerman Chair Shop 1486 Colebrook Road Lebanon, PA 17042	$1.00	*Mail order.*
Zuckermann Harpsichords, Inc. Box 121, 15 Williams Street Stonington, CT 06378	Free	*Mail orders; some instruments only display in Stonington store.*

ADDITIONAL READING

For those who want to learn more about furniture history and working with wood, here are books that I've found helpful:

Andrews, Edward Deming, and Andrews, Faith, *Religion in Wood, A Book of Shaker Furniture*, Bloomington, Ind., and London, Indiana University Press, 1971.

Coffee, Frank, *The Complete Kit House Catalog*, New York, Pocket Books, 1979.

Gibbia, S. W., *Wood Finishing and Refinishing*, rev. ed., New York, Van Nostrand Reinhold, 1954.

Gladstone, Bernard, *The Complete Home Guide to Furniture Finishing and Refinishing*, New York, Fireside, 1981.

Hayward, Charles H., *Woodwork Joints*, New York, Drake Publishers, 1970.

Higgins, Alfred, *Common-Sense Guide to Refinishing Antiques*, rev. ed., New York, Funk & Wagnalls, 1976.

Kinney, Ralph Parsons, *The Complete Book of Furniture Repair and Refinishing*, rev. ed., New York, Charles Scribner's Sons, 1971.

Kirk, John T., *American Chairs, Queen Anne and Chippendale*, New York, Alfred A. Knopf, 1972.

Miller, Edgar G., Jr., *American Antique Furniture*, Vol. I, New York, Dover Publications, 1966.

Ormsbee, Thomas H., *The Windsor Chair*, New York, Hearthside Press, 1962.

Voss, Thomas M., *Antique American Country Furniture*, Philadelphia and New York, J. B. Lippincott, 1978.

PHOTO CREDITS

ABOUT THE AUTHOR

Lynda Graham-Barber is a veteran kit builder
whose Brooklyn apartment and Vermont cabin are
both furnished almost entirely with kits that she
and her husband built themselves. A free-lance
writer, she has contributed articles to *The New
York Times*, *Ms.*, *Savvy*, *Cosmopolitan*, *Travel &
Leisure*, and other magazines and newspapers.

C.R.T. composition by Crane Typesetting Service, Inc.
Black and white printing by Murray Printing Co.
Color separation and printing by Coral Color Corp.
Produced by Kathy Grasso
Designed by Sara Eisenman